The Way I am

The Story of the Metaphysical Jesus

For too long the teachings of Jesus, hijacked by
Greek mythology, superstition, and political
ambition, were used to control the masses. Once
freed from those who pursued only power, we can
reveal one of the world's greatest transcendent
teachers, who came to teach the Way of the Divine.
Jesus lived life as the example of this Way.
Everything he did and said showed us the way. The
Way of Jesus. The Way I am.

Dr. Jim Turrell

The Way I am: The Story of the Metaphysical Jesus
By Dr. Jim Turrell
Copyright 2016 by Dr. Jim Turrell
All rights reserved

Published by HeartTalk
Costa Mesa, CA

ISBN: 978-0-9667986-3-0

Printed in the United States of America
First Printing May, 2016

This is a work of non-fiction. The ideas presented are those of
the author alone. All references to possible results to be gained
from the techniques discussed in this book relate to specific
past examples and are not necessarily representative of any
future results specific individuals may achieve.

Contents

Introduction

The Truth Will Always Be Revealed

W.A.S.P. stands for White Anglo-Saxon Protestant. I grew up a W.A.S.P. My parents were Lutherans in Chicago and Methodists in Glendale, California, where we moved in 1947. We called ourselves Christians and attended church on Christmas and Easter, except when they wanted me to go to Vacation Bible School.

I never questioned the existence of God or Jesus. My Christianity told me that God loved all of creation and Jesus loved all of us. My first religious experience in grade school consisted of an eight-week, one-hour per week after school program called Release Time Education.

The Methodist Church, across the street from Field Elementary School, hosted the program. Mrs. Redhouse, a large graceful woman who exuded kindness and creativity, taught the class. My most vivid memory? How the class made me feel. We sat facing each other at two tables in a square.

In one class, Mrs. Redhouse put a basket of apples in front of us. We all sat down and she reached across the table and pinched an apple. "Do you know what's in this apple?" she asked.

We all shook our heads. Mrs. Redhouse set the apple on a cutting board and said, "When I cut this apple in half along its meridian, you will see a miracle. A five-pointed star lives in each apple." She put the apple on the cutting board and cut it in half.

"Wow," we all said together.

"Look, see." Mrs. Redhouse passed the apple around the room.

We each looked and saw the five-pointed star and Mrs. Redhouse said, "Within in each of you is a star."

The analogy created a miracle in me. I walked home that day feeling God in my life, feeling one with a God I could trust.

Every week, Mrs. Redhouse let me drink from a source I never knew existed until she appeared in my life. An unconditional God who loved me the way I am. A God who could be trusted, never feared. A life gifted to me so I might experience love and acceptance.

Then I went to high school and suddenly heard stories about a vengeful God, an unsafe world, and a very picky Jesus, an unfriendly Christianity that felt like a shirt that didn't go with any pants I owned and a fear that felt like an indoctrination that said I should be worried, that without their God, I would never be enough. And worse, I would be left behind.

Oh well, I didn't worry, my God loved me unconditionally and protected me from fear and judgement. Besides, I loved music and so did my friends. We spent our time talking about music, sports, and school. In fact, I became so interested in music it became my career.

In the 60s through the 80s, I went to college, taught music in public school, played professionally, got married, and fathered two great kids. A few years after the birth of our daughter, my wife Jean and I started looking for a spiritual home. We went to all the popular Christian churches, read about Buddhism, Hinduism, and other Eastern approaches to spirituality, and then we found Religious Science. We went back every Sunday and each time we returned we learned a little more about how to live a life free from fear, connected to God.

I liked this spiritual approach. It challenged me to think about what I wanted my life to become and the purpose I wanted to serve.

I took all their classes. I studied Eastern and Western philosophy and religious writers including Jesus, Ralph Waldo Emerson, Thoreau, Plato, Aristotle, Jung, and Dr. Ernest Holmes, the founder of Religious Science and author of the book, *The Science of Mind*. I learned to live a life of self-reliance and in 1984, after eight years of classes and a lot of work, I became a Religious Science minister — not Scientology or Christian Science -- but Religious Science.

Religious Science defined my relationship with God and kept me on a course of study that fortified that relationship.

My study of the Bible and other scriptures wrapped itself around a *metaphysical understanding, which* carried meaning beyond the physical meaning of a verse. I viewed the Bible more as a metaphor that informed my behavior and my application of love, forgiveness, and peace.

I read the Bible and used the Metaphysical Bible Dictionary written by the Fillmores of the Unity Church to decipher the poetry and wisdom the Bible had to offer. I did not read the Bible as the literal word of God because I could never make sense of a God who encouraged fear or sanctioned punishment and death.

I did talk to others about their religious beliefs and discovered a reluctance to discuss *other* scriptures and stories about Jesus. The more I searched for the God of Unconditional Love, the higher I had to go in the academic world.

I went looking for a better explanation about the Bible and ran across a book entitled, *The Five Gospels* (published Harper San Francisco, 1993). This book combined the scholarship of the best biblical scholars from the most prestigious universities in America. These scholars met, discussed and then voted on all the statements attributed to Jesus. They colored coded their results as follows:

Red: That's Jesus!

Pink: Sounds like Jesus.

Gray: Well, maybe.

Black: There's been a mistake.

They color coded in red only 3% of the texts attributed to Jesus. They also translated the texts the way Jesus would have said it on the street, not your King James Shakespearean-style of speech. They believed Jesus did not use a self-referential style as in I am the way. More likely Jesus would have said, "The Way I am."

The New Testament scriptures most often quoted by Christian fundamentalists appeared in black or, as the scholars put it, *there's been a mistake*.

So who made the mistake?

It took over 50 years to write the New Testament. The Catholic Church finished it around 397 AD. At the time the church completed writing the New Testament, there were over 30 different stories about Jesus circulating in the Mediterranean. Saint Augustine, Saint Jerome and Saint Ambrose supervised the writing of the New Testament and then sent emissaries to find and collect all the other accounts of Jesus' life.

A few early church scholars wrote and commented about bits and pieces of the other Jesus stories. There were, however, no full copies of those stories available for research until 1945 when, in Nag Hammadi Egypt, 52 texts including a complete copy of the Gospel of Thomas surfaced along with accounts by Mary, James, and others. They called these writings the Gnostic Gospels and they portrayed a different kind of Jesus.

Most recently, the newly translated gospel of Judas gave us a radically different account of Jesus and his friend Judas. In Judas' story, Jesus recruited Judas to betray him because he knew the Roman soldiers would not recognize him.

Christian fundamentalists and the Catholic Church claim to be the exclusive judge of what Jesus said and what it means to be a devoted follower. They deny any other scriptures or interpretations different from theirs. However, I don't believe Jesus authorized the Catholic Church and/or Christian fundamentalists to be his earthly representatives.

The scholars of *The Five Gospels* did not see Jesus talking about himself in a way that portrayed his life as more important compared to anybody else. The teachings of Jesus were universal, not tribal. The

Jesus most academics talk about focuses on important areas humanity needs to study and understand. Jesus said:

Love Your Enemies

Don't React Violently

Give God What Belongs to God

Stop Looking for God Outside of Yourself

Wake Up to Your Inner Magnificence

Once You Find Your True Self, Let Go of Everything Else

Be of Service

Action Speaks Louder than Words

Nothing can Change until You Forgive

Don't Forget the Real Nature of God

Dr. Rocco Errico, who specialized in the Aramaic language and the translation of the Bible, influenced my point of view. Dr. Errico studied with George Lamsa, a world-renowned teacher who grew up in Turkey speaking Aramaic, the native conversational language of Jesus. Dr. Errico authored many books about the Bible. The Lamsa edition of the Bible is my favorite translation.

Parables, short wisdom statements, and allegory were among the tools Jesus used to open hearts and free minds. In a similar manner, this book will help readers grasp the teachings of Jesus and apply them to their lives.

The Way of Jesus will appeal to all who come seeking the truths he taught and lived.

- God is not external to your being.
- You are in God and God is in you.
- God does not play favorites.
- God does not punish anyone for making mistakes.
- You have never been separate from God.
- You cannot be left behind.

This does not mean life lacks consequence. Every circumstance, condition, and relationship you encounter corresponds to what you believe. The Way of Jesus and The Way of Cause and Effect are the same.

If you live in doubt, your doubt will become cause to your uncertainty. If you live in fear, your fear will become cause to your sense of isolation. If you react with anger, your anger will attract angry people.

God does not know you separate from itself. God does not judge you. God responds to what you believe and animates that belief, which creates your personal sense of what life feels like.

Your God-Self is whole, perfect, and complete. Your intellectual and egocentric self, however, experiences a less than perfect self, one that is incomplete and unfulfilled.

Additional confusion surrounds Jesus because the Romans who converted to Christianity wrote of Jesus as a Demigod, half human and half God possessed of supernatural powers. These later translators of the Bible saw Jesus the same way they saw their Roman Gods. Hercules, the son of Zeus became a heroic Demigod. Jesus, the son of Mary and God similarly possessed powers that proclaimed him a supernatural healer.

The early disciples of Jesus did not write about him that way. Instead, they saw Jesus as the example of humanity's potential, not the exception. More likely Jesus would have said, "…he who believes in me, the works that I do, he will do also; and greater works than these he will do; because I go to the Father." These are not the words of a self-proclaimed Demigod. They are the words of a great teacher who found a personal sense of authority in his connection with his Divine Father. The teacher Jesus inspired his disciples to follow his example. The philosopher Jesus shared his wisdom and helped his disciples develop compassion and wisdom.

The Way of Jesus and the Way of Love mirror a way of life that puts God first. His message encourages you to break free from your traditions and discover a spiritual storehouse ready to open

and tap. Welcome to the Real World! The Way of
Jesus!

"To think of Jesus as being different from other men is to misunderstand his mission and purpose in life. He was a way-shower, and proved his way to be a correct one!"
—Dr. Ernest Holmes, *Science of Mind*

Chapter 1
The Way of Jesus

The Stories, Wisdom and Sayings of Jesus

I asked a psychologist friend of mine to explain P.T.S.D., Post Traumatic Stress Disorder. She said, "It's like, if I invited you to come to my backyard and every time you went to sit down, I pulled the chair out from under you. If I did that enough, you would start to look behind yourself fearful that the chair would not be there when you went to sit down."

Too much of the world is looking behind itself, wondering who pulled their life out from under them. Stressed and in states of disorder, people lose confidence and trust. Their fear epidemic, they panic and struggle to manage their circumstances, afraid to breathe, looking out of the corner of their eye for a different way to live.

There is a different way to live and you can trust it. You can use the Way of Jesus to control how you think. Even after thousands of years, the Way of Jesus still provides a proactive approach that builds trust and confidence in your relationship with God. This Way of Jesus powered by love, forgiveness, and faith shows you how to apply truth to power.

Jesus applied truth to power by declaring his trust in a spiritual authority that said…

> *"Have trust in God. I swear to you, those who say to this mountain, 'Up with you and into the sea!' and do not waver in their conviction, but trust that what they say will happen, that's the way it will be. This is why I keep telling you, trust that you will receive everything you pray and ask for, and that's the way it will turn out. And when you stand up to pray, if you are holding anything against anyone, forgive them, so your Father in heaven may forgive your misdeeds." Mark 11:22-25*

Pray, ask, trust, and be willing to forgive. Would you do these things if you knew that your forgiveness and faith would move mountains? This same kind of trust echoes what happens within the seed when it commands the soil to help it grow. Once you plant a seed-idea into your mentality, the consciousness you accumulate (your spiritual soil) will activate the essential elements and command your growth.

Mind and the soil are the same. Whatever you put into your mind grows. Productive seed-ideas, planted in soil prepared to receive them, achieve fruition, moving whatever stands in their way to manifest their goal. However, an unprepared mind, full of weeds and resentments, chokes your desires and cuts short your opportunities. These weeds come from the seeds of discontent, planted by negative opinions and judgments. These seeds, stored in your subconscious mind, wait to be stimulated when you have a negative reaction.

Your conscious mind plants negative seeds when anger, fear, worry, or concern capture your attention. This stimulates the negative seeds in your subconscious mind, which grows the weeds of discontent that strangle your enthusiasm. In fact, the majority of all discontent comes from memorized and stored subconscious reactions that wait to be stimulated in response to the conditions you encounter.

Who would plant such seeds? It depends on how susceptible you are to the negative influence of others. You are not born with negative tendencies. You learn negativity through the observation of how others react in their efforts to control their environment. Moment by moment, day after day, year by year your optimism fades with every negative seed planted.

Listen to how Jesus cautions his disciples about the condition of their consciousness when they think.

"This sower went out to sow. While he was sowing, some seed fell along the path, and the birds came and ate it up. Other seed fell on rocky ground where there wasn't much soil, and it came up right away because the soil had no depth. When the sun came up it was scorched, and because it has not roots it withered. Still other seed fell among thorns came up and choked them. Other seed fell on good earth and started producing fruit: one part had a yield of one hundred, another a yield of sixty, and third a yield of thirty. Anyone here with two ears had better listen." Matthew 13:3-9

A hardened heart will close your mind. A life with no depth will die in the heat of despair, dismayed by weed-like thoughts that minimize and marginalize desire. However, if you are receptive to a richer and more successful life, *your knowledge will become the authority of your word.* Accumulate a greater authority and your life will manifest and receive an abundant crop of love and creative initiative.

The Way of Jesus uses logic to clarify the message. I went to college in the mid-sixties. I remember the confusion created by negative scenarios concerned with my future. Like many of my fellow students, temptation closed my eyes and focused my energies on controlling outcomes instead of shaping the future. I did not know the difference between a reactive thought and a proactive thought. Instead, I fell under the spell of an egocentric nature, overloaded with too many reactions that made me unavailable to my potential. The more I stayed unavailable, the more I found myself trapped in my needs, worried and afraid, the victim of a conditional life.

Are you ready to wake up? Jesus would say…

"Listen and try to understand. It's not what goes into the mouth that defiles a person; rather, it's what comes out of the mouth that defiles a person." Matthew 15:10, 11

When you think a self-defeating thought and bring it forward through your words, you give it legs and it runs away with you. It literally causes you to take the wrong off-ramp and get lost on the way to your real life.

Have you ever given thought to a new desire and then immediately thought, "There's no way that will happen." Human ignorance killed your dream and took you away from the pathway of discovery necessary to find the real you.

The Way of Jesus empowers faith and uses the knowledge of God's creative presence to neutralize negative thoughts. Grasp this understanding and do not let your imagination compromise your possibilities. If you ignore your Creator and defer to a world of competition and small-mindedness, you will limit your potential.

My wife and I went to see the movie *Hidden Figures*. It told the story of a group of African-American women working in the south in the 60s at the National Aeronautics and Space Administration. Congress created NASA to put a satellite into space and then put a man into orbit around the earth. These African-American women, talented at complicated calculations, suffered major discrimination, yet they contributed their mathematical talents without complaint, patiently waiting for their opportunity to rise and be recognized. It took years for that recognition to happen, and it finally did at the 2017 Academy Awards when one of these women, Katherine Johnson, over 90 years old, rolled out in a wheelchair to a wild and enthusiastic audience. What would Jesus have said about Katherine Johnson?

Jesus would have said, "Katherine,

"That's why I tell you: Don't fret about your life—what you're going to eat and drink—or about your body—what you're going to wear. There is more to living than food and clothing, isn't there? Take a look at the birds of the sky: they don't plant or harvest, or gather into barns. Yet your heavenly Father feeds them. You're worth more than they, aren't you? Can any of you add one hour to life by fretting about it?" Matthew 6:25

Jesus observed humanity. He knew worry created the illusion of that your life would never be enough, a kind of worry that stimulates huge amounts of uncertainty. Jesus knew worry begs the question: How can I not worry? Just look at my life. Everything I worry about seems to come true.

When the power of fear drives the misuse of our lives, we fail to see worry as a choice.

Worry is a choice. Fear is a choice. Uncertainty is a choice. All are motivated by the ego's need to control and dominate. This choice controls how our reactions blind us to the opportunity to love and cripples us with doubt that plants a seed that says, *maybe we are not enough.* If you stay focused on this problem in a state of worry, you will recreate the problem in every area of your life. What you think and feel, you create.

Thoughts and feelings create your experience and create the direction in which you move. This makes people angry. The Way of Jesus teaches you how to choose a new way to think. Listen to how Jesus' logic interrupts the spell and seeks to awaken humanity to a spiritual truth. Jesus says…

> *"…in fact to those who have more will be given, and from those who don't have, even what they seem to have will be taken away." Luke 8:18*

This stark saying tells us we must be careful in how we listen to those eager to plant seeds of doubt, worry, or fear. We must pay attention to how our disappointments throw us off the abundance train. We must see the train of thought fear creates and how it takes us in the wrong direction and causes us to scuffle with life.

If we begin to believe we are lost, limited, or unworthy, we will create a state of mind where even that which we have God will take from us. Therefore, it is important to move in the direction of what you want, not what you don't want. Things like credit reports and critical reviews can be institutional words of disapproval that have lasting effects because they appear to limit the scope and range of your dreams and desires. Keep in mind: these criticisms are the seeds of future discontents.

In 1968, I began my teaching career as a student teacher at Foshay Junior High School on the fringe of inner city LA. Foshay, built for 600 students, had over 1,200 enrolled. My first teaching assignment, a general music class on the third floor just above a math class on the second floor, meant that I could not make any sounds that would disturb the math class below me.

I had 36 students in the class who were there because they didn't want to take band, orchestra, or choir, and the State of California required them to have at least a semester of music in their junior high school experience. This meant that I had to create lesson plans that made music interesting and fun. Mrs. Washington, my master teacher, said I had two weeks to work with the students before her first visit. She did encourage me to make discipline my first aim and to come up with a strategy that would create respect and interest at the same time.

My lessons had to be exciting and entertaining enough to motivate my students. I created 15 different experiences that I kept on hand in case one of my lessons did not work. However, I failed to factor in interruptions, disputes, or kids who needed extra attention. The first three days were a disaster and I began to think, "Maybe I should do something else."

On the fourth day Mrs. Washington paid me a surprise visit. I executed my lesson and used all 15 experiences. During the class, two kids started a fight, messages from the office interrupted twice, and three needy students wanted all my attention. Despite completing all 15 experiences, I still doubted. "Am I cut out to do this work?" I thought.

The bell rang. The students left. I sighed. Mrs. Washington handed me a long list of things I succeeded in teaching despite all the interruptions and distractions. "Good job," she said and walked out of the room.

If your confidence disappears and you stop trusting your effort, no doubt you will lose your self-assurance and focus on what you think is the failure. I impressed Mrs. Washington with my preparedness. Despite all the interruptions, she did not disapprove of my methods. She saw my strengths and helped me see the value of my effort.

Critics who focus on weaknesses to correct or improve forget that God did not create you to fail.

Who loves weakness? The critic loves weakness; they can't see anything but weakness. They don't inspire; they correct.

Who loves strength? The teacher loves strength because that's what the teacher builds upon! They inspire by suggesting ways to improve.

Critics are slaves to what they hate and what they love, correction. Teachers who come from strength have an unfettered dedication to one idea, the advancement of their students.

> *"No one can be a slave to two masters. No doubt that slave will either hate one and love the other, or be devoted to one and disdain the other. You can't be enslaved to both God and a bank account!" Matthew 6:24*

In my first teaching assignment at Foshay Junior High School, I was fortunate to learn from a wonderful math and drum teacher, Charlotte Fowler. Charlotte, a broad-shouldered woman, would do almost anything to help her students succeed. Her classroom was on the ground level of a three-story building built in the '30s with large windows that swiveled open.

In the morning, I stood on the front steps of the school, assigned to encourage students to get to class on time. I noticed one of Charlotte's math students, enrolled in her afterschool drum class, walking too slow to make her math class on time. I yelled, "Anthony, hurry up." At the same time, Charlotte was motioning Anthony to her window. This young man could not afford to be tardy. One more and he would be cut from the drum class.

He approached the window and Charlotte reached down and grabbed the back of his pants, and pulled him in just as the tardy bell began to ring. This example of Charlotte's love of teaching and love of her students inspired me.

Jesus, like Charlotte, pulled humanity through the windows of opportunity. Those who observed Jesus' love would emulate his example and use his type of affirmative voice to energize the Law of Attraction. The Way of Jesus, applied through prayer, pulls others through their conditions and circumstances.

What inspires you? Can you describe the feelings you want more of in your life, as if they were already so? Do you take time to imagine how it would feel to live the life you want? A cautionary note: Do not envision your life like a movie. Instead, see your life from the inside looking out serving your highest desire, a vision active and expressive in reaction to your feelings and thoughts.

Jesus characterized inspiration and brilliantly spoke the following analogy. Jesus said…

"No one lights a lamp and covers it with a pot or puts it under a bed; rather, one puts it on a lamp stand, so that those who come in can see the light. After all, there is nothing hidden that won't be brought to light, nor secreted away that won't be made known and exposed." Luke 8:16

First light, then form. Light takes form, then deserts form. You light a lamp and put it out into the open so all can see. Your light illumines your path.

Those who hide their light—the nature of who they truly are—will not find their way. We must become transparent to ourselves and see the way life intends us to live.

See through your problem and the problem ceases to exist. You have the authority to affirm your thoughts alive and worry-free. If faced with an unsolvable problem, say aloud: "I don't know what I'm doing here, but something within me does."

Here is a brief Affirmative Prayer you can apply to the presence of a problem in your life.

Today God moves my life into a new awareness of my eternal good. Whatever I saw as a problem I now dismiss as a distorted perception that I now change by seeing my Divine Creator and myself as one. The nature of God's Love casts out my fear and opens my eyes to a greater presence of peace and fulfillment. Thank you, God, for all my blessings. Released, my word is now the manifest expression of my life! AND SO IT IS.

To Ask is Power

"Rest assured: everyone who asks receives; everyone who seeks, finds; and for the one who knocks it is opened. Matthew 7:9-11

The word *ask* represents three mysteries: The ability to know what we want, where to find it, and how to attract it. If we keep telling ourselves that we don't know what we want, we disconnect from God. When you know you're connected, you know the way.

People who lack faith live in the mystery and refuse to act upon the opportunities presented. Their disbelief reflects itself in their fear of rejection and their unwillingness to disturb the status quo. If they ask for too much, they will be disappointed. If they keep a low profile and behave themselves, maybe some small crumb will fall their way.

Jesus understood those who did not believe in their own authority and their own inherent right to an abundant life. The unbeliever's life always looks like a sacrifice. They see themselves as victims suffering in a world of have-nots, mystified by those that have what they want.

Jesus amplifies this message by affirming an important truth. Jesus said…

"In fact, to those who have, more will be given, and then some; and from those who don't have, even what they do have will be taken away." *Matthew 13:12*

Could it be that the same Law that imprisons me could also set me free?

The way of Jesus mirrors the Law of Attraction, and the ability to use the Law creates the life you want to live, which you cannot do by yourself.

"The Son can do nothing of himself." John 5:19

A connected sense of oneness with a Universal Divine empowers each to cooperate and share this world. This nullifies the drive for dominance and competition.

The individual does not create his or her life; rather, the individual emancipates life, accepting responsibility to dismiss his or her own personal fear and doubt. When you dismiss thoughts that separate you from a peaceful life and invoke a conscious thought that connects you with a universal peace, you activate a world that follows your lead. The Way of Jesus functions like a mental tractor, preparing the soil for the kind of seed-thoughts that grow in a world starving for the kind of food that will strengthen its resolve to live in peace.

What you consume mentally determines how you engage life. Your success depends on how you embody the Law of Attraction and use it in your everyday life. A negative mental diet depletes your resolve and limits your view, of the world. What you cannot see from your own view you tend to notice in the way others see the world. This is why hypocrites notice the mistakes in others but cannot see it in themselves.

"Why do you notice the sliver in your friend's eye, but overlook the timber in your own?" Matthew 7:3-5

Break free from your bondage of limitation and death and remove the perception that separates you from the Divine. Affirm your oneness with the Divine. Create a new perception that sees you prosperous and rich.

"One can't enter a strong person's house and take it by force without tying his hands. Then one can loot the house." Thomas 35

In this quote from the Gospel of Thomas, Jesus attests to the kind of internal voice of hostility that accompanies certain kinds of thoughts and feelings. The thought of limitation ties your hands and enables those around you to loot your most precious resource, your faith. A con artist hypnotizes his or her victim and steals their wealth. Internal con artists such as betrayal, death, and expectation, are each a crook that steals your confidence, delays your willingness to try again, and inflates your fear.

The separated person lives in a reality that overstates the importance of fear. When you live from fear you will never know peace. Affirmative Prayer dismisses fear and restates the intention to live from Peace. Fear window-shops for peace and tries to buy the experience for the same reason that fear-driven people buy tickets to amusement parks, for the distraction.

The Law of Attraction can operate from either fear or faith. If you operate from both fear and faith at the same time, it creates confusion and distraction. You must choose from whence you come, fear or faith.

The Law of Attraction, coming from the presence of faith, creates a constructive life that responds to your affirmative thoughts and feels right. In the Bible, Jesus referred to this as "Heaven's imperial rule."

"For Heaven's imperial rule is like a proprietor who went out the first thing in the morning to hire workers for his vineyard. After agreeing with the workers for a silver coin a day he sent them into his vineyard.

"And coming out around 9 a.m. he saw others loitering in the marketplace and he said to them. 'You go into the vineyard too, and I'll pay you whatever is fair." So they went.

"Around noon, he went out again, and at 3 p.m., and repeated the process. About 5 p.m. he went out and found others loitering about and says to them, 'Why did you stand around here idle the whole day?'

"They reply, 'Because no one hired us.'

"He tells them, 'You go into the vineyard as well.'

"When evening came, the owner of the vineyard tells his foreman: 'Call the workers and pay them their wages starting with those hired last and ending with those hired first.'

"Those hired at 5 p.m. came up and received a silver coin each. Those hired first approached thinking they would receive more. But they also got a silver coin apiece. 'These guys hired last worked only an hour but you have made them equal to us who did most of the work during the heat of the day.'

"In response, he said to one of them, 'Look, pal, did I wrong you? You did agree with me for a silver coin, didn't you? Take your wage and get out! I intend to treat the one hired last the same way I treat you. Is there some law forbidding me to do with my money as I please? Or is your eye filled with envy because I am generous?'

"The last will be first and the first last." Matthew 20:1-16

People compare their lives to others and complain, "The world's not fair." And in fact, it isn't.

Dr. Eric Butterworth in his book *Spiritual Economics* says, "The world doesn't owe you a living, but the Universe does." The Law of Attraction does not play favorites. It works for everyone. NO ONE IS LEFT BEHIND. If you're angry because someone received more than you, the Law doesn't care. Your anger is the consequence for how you value your life in comparison with others.

When you get the Way of Jesus, you will stop comparing your blessings with others; you will stop trying to impress the world; and you will start working with the Universe to manifest the life God created you to live.

Imagine a way of life that uses a SELF-DEFINING TRUTH to create everything it wants. The Law of Attraction creates as you believe. Most people do not see it.

> *"It will not come by watching for it. It will not be said, 'Look, here!' or 'Look, there!' Rather, the Father's imperial rule is spread out upon the earth, and people don't see it."* Thomas 113

Why does God hide this truth? Why not just show it to everyone and let everyone get on with living life?

No one can understand a God that would withhold because God does not withhold. We do. We withhold our attention, our feelings, our thoughts and our dreams.

When did you last take the time to spend more than an hour visualizing the life you want to live? People do not think this way because they've been taught to believe that taking time to imagine your good will not result in achieving your goals.

People believe that solving their problems will lead them to happiness. Worse yet, they believe it defines how much good they can have.

I found the Way of Jesus in the early 70s when I started studying metaphysics. The study of the Law of Attraction helped magnetize my life and drew to me the perfect resources and teachers that explained the Way of Jesus.

My parents found the Way of Jesus in the late '60's and my Dad, who lived to be 97, used the Way to live a rich and full life. The Way of Jesus does not help you get money. The Way of Jesus animates the conscious thought about being rich, creating an awakened life wealthy with friends, family, faith and fortune.

"How difficult it is for those who have money to enter God's domain!" Mark 10: 23

"It's easier for a camel to squeeze through a needle's eye than for a wealthy person to get into God's Domain." Mark 10: 25

The scholars of the Five Gospels knew that Jesus loved surprise endings and exaggeration. Jesus compares the difficulty of living a life of spiritual principles versus a life of those who think that they can buy peace of mind and happiness. The lessons of Jesus are important because they compel you to live in spiritual principles that challenge the world's view of how most people think.

What we think, we animate. What we animate, we experience. What we experience; we tend to memorialize. What we memorialize, mezmorises us and we cast a spell which becomes the problem that hurt us, the condition that kill us, or the circumstance which limits us. Humanity has become convinced that their problem is cause to their experience. Jesus, a master teacher of cause and effect, untangled that web and freed those trapped in their human memory.

"I like your Christ, I do not like your Christians. Your Christians are so unlike your Christ."
—Mahatma Gandhi

Chapter 2
Ten Cause and Effect Teachings of Jesus

Cause and Effect Teachings

The teachings of Jesus are a Cause and Effect teaching. The Way of Jesus instructs and engages the whole brain. The Way of Jesus uses drama to capture attention and direct the student's focus on outrageous contradictions. Shocked and taken aback, the student's reaction begs an explanation. "What do you mean, love your enemies and pray for your persecutors? Why would I do that?" Engaged, the student demands an answer that becomes the Way of Jesus.

The answer in this case explains the benefit of the first step of a Cause and Effect teaching, to connect the student with Cause, also known as God. Then it compares this sacred connection to a general rule of spiritual logic that shows—not explains—that God does not play favorites. This provocative idea questions the motive and intent of all who are listening and challenges their understanding of life.

It literally slams the student's mentality into a contradiction that questions the value of a belief shaped by tradition. This reveals to the student a new way to think and introduces a new influence which shapes the student's logic similar to the way Einstein's Theory of Relativity showed us how mass and energy were interchangeable, that the temporary nature of form, once complete, would deconstruct back into energy.

Thus the student can see how their thought inspires new ways of behaving that shapes their energy into a new form of life. In other words, *thoughts become things.* This begs another question.

What do we possess that can translate raw energy into form? This translator must be able to learn the language of the Divine and translate it into feelings and ideas that motivate a willingness to explore the unknown, then create a consciousness that activates a new belief based on new assumptions that so dramatically changes our way of thinking that it produces a new perception. The student at last sees what he or she seeks to find.

The 10 examples that follow show the genius of Jesus, the teacher. They grab your attention, correct your perception and show you the way of God's Love, the Way of Jesus!

Number One - Love Your Enemies

"Love your enemies and pray for your persecutors. You'll then become children of your Father in the heavens. God causes the sun to rise on both the bad and the good, and sends rain on both the just and the unjust. Tell me, if you love those who love you, why should you be commended for that? Even the toll collectors do as much, don't they?" Matthew 5:44-46

In the Way of Jesus, you must learn to love and forgive. Principles are powerful because they center your attention on how you think, feel, and behave in the moment. If you focus on fear or uncertainty, you will shut down your capacity to be willing and receptive. Instead, you will spend your thoughts, feelings, and behavior on being willful and demanding.

Fear causes your egocentric nature to control and dominate how you react to the conditions and circumstances you encounter. Love causes your willing and receptive nature to stay in the moment and allow the creation of absolute goodness.

This works because you choose to focus on a Principle and not a condition. When a Principle like love defines your behavior, it resolves circumstances and creates new possibilities.

A Principle refers to the way a law works. The Law of Gravity works the same for a good person and a bad person. The Law of Attraction, a universal Principle that works the same for everyone, emotionally validates what you draw to yourself.

For example, if there are some things you hate about your job, it appears inevitable that you will continue to have to deal with what you hate. Jesus says, "Love your enemies," or your feelings of anger, resentment and guilt will weaken your ability to focus on what you want.

These bad feelings are a low frequency signal to the world that what you hate matters. Conversely, feelings of joy, gratitude, and love send a high-frequency signal to the world that what you love and are grateful for matters. God plays no favorites. God shows up by being an equal-opportunity employer.

The sun rises on both the bad and the good. The Way of Jesus makes it easy to love your friends. Your choice to live the Way of Jesus makes it wise to love your enemies. Wisdom makes friends with circumstances and does not attach itself to outcomes. When you take away the sting of unmet expectations, you have no reason to be disappointed.

A girl, featured on Oprah, shared that her boss fired her that morning and that at first she felt upset and disappointed. Then she woke up. She realized she did not like her job anymore and that her boss did the right thing in letting her go. In fact, she thanked him for hiring and firing her. She changed her mind, forgave herself for the wrong point of view, and moved forward with what she wanted to do.

Her new way of thinking activated the Law of Attraction. The loss of her job enabled her to activate her mentality to start looking for new opportunities. Once your mind knows what you want, it can identify the opportunities that are right before you. Thus you see what you are looking for.

Number Two – Don't React Violently

"Don't react violently against the one who is evil: when someone slaps you on the right cheek, turn the other as well. When someone wants to sue you for your shirt, let that person have your coat along with it. Further, when anyone conscripts you for one mile, go an extra mile. Give to the one who begs from you." Matthew 5:39-42

If you are going to grow up, you must give up reacting to those who hurt, harm or seek to diminish your presence. The Way of Jesus clarifies the Law of Attraction, being tough on those who behave poorly and equally tough on those who turn into the very thing they fear.

When we experience life, we tend not to remember what happened. We are more inclined to remember how we felt. Jesus seemed to know this and taught his disciples to avoid their habitual tendency to react from their memory in a violent manner.

These reactions are *memorized responses* fueled by emotional recall brought up from the subconscious storehouse of *things that protect me when I feel threatened.* In my profession, violent reactions are loops of helplessness and, when triggered, go into expression without one having to think. They are so automatic that they can override any good thoughts, unless those good thoughts and feelings are solidly in place.

This begs the question: How do you put those good triggers into place so they fire the right signals and attract the right results? How do you neutralize the old triggers?

My last teaching assignment, before I became a minister, was at a middle school that had five principals in six years. Successful schools provide a continuity that builds trust and cooperation. A new principal every year will not build the trust and cooperation a successful school requires. The same idea manifests in a lack of cooperation and trust when we still live in our memorized reactions pulling triggers we can't see. These memorized responses live in our emotional memory until a teacher shows up and wakes us up. Growth, cooperation, and trust are the byproducts of a spiritual commitment that starts trust.

In my last year of teaching, I became the union rep for our school, and on one occasion, I expressed to our "new" principal that I thought his requests were beyond the scope of what our teachers had time to do.

He asked to see me in private the next morning. I walked into his office. He told me to sit on the couch. I sat down and immediately sunk into the couch so far I could barely stand up without rolling off the couch on my knees. I sunk in to the couch and at the same time he brought a chair from around his desk and sat right in front of me. He could block any effort I might make to stand up.

First words out of his mouth were, "You will never again talk to me the way you addressed me yesterday after our faculty meeting. You are a blah, blah, blah and I don't respect you or like you."

I went into an equally offensive mode and fired back, "You little blah, blah, blah." Then I got to my feet and stormed out of his office. I fumed for several days and finally called my minister, Rev. Les.

He listened to my story, nodded his head, and said, "First thing you must do, and I know you are not going to like this, is forgive him and yourself. Second thing we must do is pray for his complete success."

I sat for a few moments stunned by his advice. "I can't pray for his success. That little blah, blah, blah."

Les stopped me and said, "We must change your perception of him, otherwise he, or another just like him, will be in your life until you change your mind."

I did not understand. "Explain this to me."

Les said, "This person lives within you. He symbolizes a belief you have to release. We must use affirmative prayer to create the consciousness where this belief can no longer operate within your life."

Les explained Cause and Effect, "Your mentality reacts because it remembers the threat his authority symbolizes. You need a new idea of love and acceptance. Jim, you must release the old belief you hold about this principal and declare him a complete success. Once we write the prayer, forgive him and declare him a success, your Spiritual Self will release him."

I did not believe at first; however, I did commit to do the prayer work for this principal's success and my ability to release him. I wrote the prayer and Les helped me edit it. I read it every night before I went to bed and every morning when I got up. Two weeks into my prayer therapy the principal asked to meet with the faculty in an emergency meeting the next morning. We gathered for the meeting and the principal announced that he was taking a supervisor's position in another district and would be leaving next week. He thanked us all for our support and walked out of the room.

I went home feeling good because my prayers for his success worked and he was no longer a prisoner in my mind. Violence, physical or mental, serves to amplify fear and resentment.

Jesus said, "*When anyone conscripts you for one mile, go an extra mile.*" I went the extra mile, and that made all the difference.

Number Three – Give God What Belongs to God

"Give the emperor what belongs to the emperor; give God what belongs to God." Thomas 100:2

The world we live in consists of thoughts and feelings held in memory by each person. Jung called this the collective unconscious. I call it the Race Mind: the collective emotional memory of the entire human race held in the mental memory of each human. This emotional memory, scripted with reactions with what to say and do, protects you and seeks to control the circumstances you encounter. It speaks with an internal voice that sounds appropriate and God-like.

Sometimes people ask me how to distinguish the voice of God versus the critical voice that makes them feel righteous, not happy.

Who's speaking and what do they want? The ego is a strong voice that always seeks to judge, compare, weigh, measure, and value character and meaning. God's voice does none of that. God's voice speaks only of love and goodness.

God says act, think, and feel as love would. Love is the ultimate authority of how life will turn out. Give God and life all your love, and give to the world what belongs to the world. In this way, your life becomes an act of trust and happens without effort, sure of where God lives—in everything and everyone. Informed by your oneness, unity becomes your way and living life in Love becomes your purpose. Then reality can unfold within your life.

The emperor demands righteous indignation. God offers love and forgiveness.

Once upon a time, I wanted to build a swimming pool. I searched far and wide for the best person to do the job. I found him and he drew up the plans. He finished building the pool and I hired another person to install the concrete deck. All was good until I noticed the pool was losing water too fast. There must be a leak. I bought a stethoscope and tried to find the leak by going around the pool, listening like a doctor listens for a heartbeat. No heartbeat. No leak.

Next thing to do was remove the deck. I rented a concrete saw, jackhammer, and a dump truck. I put a red bandana around my head and cut the deck into squares. I hooked up the compressor and the jackhammer and loaded the squares into the dump truck. I drove 25 miles to the dump, a mile-wide deep sand pit with a steep road just wide enough for the truck. I paid my money at the top of the pit and drove to the bottom where I was told I could dump my concrete.

I backed up the truck and read the instruction on how to raise the bed of the truck. I followed the instructions and the bed began to rise. I listened for the concrete to slide off the bed of the truck. No sound could I hear. I got out of the truck and looked up to the top where I drove in and saw three men with binoculars pointed at me. I waved. They waved back. I walked to the back of the truck to see why the concrete had not slide off the bed. I noticed the chains holding the tailgate of the truck and the concrete was pressing against it. Standing behind the truck, I started to remove the chains and then it struck me! *If I remove these chains all this concrete will fall on me.* Then I looked up and saw those three men were still watching me.

What could have altered my state of mind to the point of such carelessness? Righteous indignation stood behind that truck; outrage drove it; and anger rented those tools. All that emotion belongs to the emperor. Feeling your emotions is normal. The abnormal reaction comes when you see yourself as the victim and blame God or Life for the problem.

If I knew then what I know now, I would dismiss my emotions and tell myself to focus on being peaceful. I would affirm my inherent authority to declare myself to be the agent of love and walk through the episode instead of stopping to become indignant, outraged and angry.

Number Four – Stop Looking for God Outside of Yourself

"It will not come by watching for it. It will not be said, 'Look, here! or Look, there!' Rather, the Father's imperial rule is spread out upon the earth, and people don't see it." Thomas 113:2

In this statement, the Way of Jesus tells you where to look for God everywhere. God in all is all.

Ralph Waldo Emerson wrote, "Being is the **vast affirmative**, excluding negation, self-balanced, and swallowing up all relations..." Go within and you will find the primordial life that connects you with all.

Who goes within? You think it true that the idea of God's presence lives as the essence of all form or does it go unnoticed? An often stated popular concept concerns a power opposed to God's presence. Confusion rules when you cannot figure out why God would create a representational power greater than Itself.

My God breathes in a world of oneness. Others live in a world of opposites. If there is an up, there must be a down; an in, an out; an over, an under; a good, a bad; a wrong, a right. A world filled with duality impossible to escape, locked in the experience of sight, sound, smell, taste, and touch, convinces people of their limitations and lack.

However, we possess the ability to abstract a larger invisible essence if we exercise the authority of our imagination.

A school of Greek philosophers, known as the Atomists, believed that small invisible particles made up the physical presence of all life. They believed this even though they had no physical proof. Of course, it turned out to be true and science today uses their concepts.

Where did they get the idea?

If you were to ask a mathematician where certain advanced equations came from, they would tell you the imagination. Even Einstein admitted that imagination superseded the importance of knowledge.

Humanity underestimates the consciousness it possesses to imagine a greater life. Try saying this aloud:

"My life is a vast affirmative excluding all negation, self-balanced and swallowing up all relations."

How would your life be different if you were part of a vast affirmative? Take time each day and gently tap at the center of your chest where your heart lives and repeat the preceding affirmation.

The evidence of our unity with life presents itself in every relationship, condition, and circumstance we experience. Jesus said, *"The Father's imperial rule is spread out upon the earth, and people don't see it."* The invisible appears when we prepare ye the way, the Way of Jesus. Prepare ye the way of Love. Prepare ye the way of Peace. Prepare yourself to receive Love, and you will. Prepare yourself to be Peaceful, and you will. "Prepare" means choose love and choose peace daily. Choose them as your way to behave and receive.

Number Five – Wake Up to Your Inner Magnificence

"Heaven's imperial rule is like leaven which a woman took and concealed in fifty pounds of flour until it was all leavened." Matthew 13:33

In early Judaic traditions leaven indicated corruption. However, here, Jesus uses leaven as a metaphor for Heaven's imperial rule. This means Heaven's state of mind conceals itself from our view, until we get the ears to hear it and the eyes to see it.

The way of Jesus becomes obvious when you realize that you must leaven your thoughts with awareness and have faith that the Way of Jesus operates 24/7.

The Law of Attraction is just like gravity, automatic. If we fail to think the productive thought, we will attract the non-productive response and stand to lose even what we already have. Turn to the fulfilling feelings you hold sacred. Combine this with gratitude and keep a log of that vast sea of love that calls you to act in God's favor and change everything that needs changing. Gratitude, like leaven, causes life to rise to the occasion of your love.

Number Six – Once You Find Your True Self, Let Go of Everything Else

"Heaven's imperial rule is like treasure hidden in a field: when someone finds it, that person covers it up again, and out of sheer joy goes and sells every last possession and buys that field.

"Again, Heaven's imperial rule is like some trader looking for beautiful pearls. When that merchant finds one priceless pearl, he sells everything he owns and buys it." Matthew 13:44-45

This is a great example of how we must treat our egos. It is by no mistake that the ego is known as the trickster and that it can fool you into believing the worst-case scenario, following the least-productive path, and acting in the lowest possible way.

Revenge, resentment, and doubt are its tools and the ego uses them to construct a state of mind, constantly seeking to predict outcomes, control situations, and manipulate relationships. But be true to yourself and you can release the possessive and become the owner of a seamless existence.

The Way of Jesus compares the seamless life to the seamless robe, a garment we possess but do not acknowledge. The ego and emperor live in the gap, naked and separate from the sacred and seamless authority of God. Their life, torn apart by need and desperation, demands recognition for their plight, not their pupose.

Our perfection demands a consistent and persistent use of visualization. This sets the Law of Attraction into motion, animating new subconscious thoughts that point at our potential, not our problem.

To enter this land of unconditioned potential, you must get past the superficial and into the deep end of your heart. This affects the kinds of changes the heart yearns for.

On the other hand, if you say this doesn't work, you command the law to not work. So it works by appearing not to work. This is not a punishment. This is consequence.

By using the Law of Attraction to think with purpose, you create a sense of wonder and receptivity in your everyday experience of life.

There was a time when I was twelve and sold toffee-flavored peanuts door to door to earn my way to a week of wonder at Camp Fox on Catalina Island.

My purpose at twelve, thirteen, and fourteen pointed at one thing, to live that adventure in pure discovery mode every summer with my band of brothers. The sound of the ocean and cool crisp mornings woke me to another day of swimming, hiking, laughing, peanut butter sandwiches, games, and friendship. For one week every summer I found my true self and let go of everything else.

The true self hides in a field of wonder just outside of our awareness. To gain access, give up all else and buy that field. It awaits your discovery.

Number Seven – Be of Service

"There was a man going from Jerusalem down to Jericho when he fell into the hands of robbers. They stripped him, beat him up, and went off, leaving him half dead. Now by coincidence a priest was going down that road; when he caught sight of him, he went out of his way to avoid him. In the same way, when a Levite came to the place, he took one look at him and crossed the road to avoid him. But this Samaritan who was traveling that way came to where he was and was moved to pity at the sight of him. He went up to him and bandaged his wounds, pouring olive oil and wine on them. He hoisted him onto his own animal, brought him to an inn, and looked after him. The next day he took out two silver coins, which he gave to the

innkeeper, and said, 'look after him, and on my way back I'll reimburse you for any extra expense you have had.'" Matthew 13:30-35

Service and generosity are the same. There are many occasions in the reported life of Jesus where he emphasizes the importance of generosity and the willingness to help another human being reclaim his or her life. When you help another, you help yourself. We are all one within the One. We are all connected. The Universal nature of God's love does not exclude anyone.

This beautiful story is a surprise to most because the Samaritan not only helps the wounded man, he makes sure the care for the man continues. I believe in the basic goodness of humanity. I believe that each person has the capacity to love and care for anyone in need. Perhaps Mother Theresa is the most well-known advocate of helping those in need. I don't believe she could have done what she did if it were not for the Law of Attraction.

Through the act of extending selfless service she drew to her vast amounts of wealth, materials, and people to put her vision into play. She held the idea of her service to humanity as her reality and acted in complete faith.

We must forever nurture our relationship with God, for every relationship we engage in will reflect our love of God based on our acts of generosity and service. Life doesn't keep score, it keeps tabs. As we engage, we either emancipate or encapsulate our potential. One way leads to freedom, the other to separation from source. Affirm:

God, the source and supply of all my good, forever feeds my creative mind with more and more ways to express, receive, and multiply my good.

Number Eight – Action Speaks Louder than Words

"You'll know who they are by what they produce. Since when do people pick grapes from thorns or figs from thistles?" Matthew 7:16

In the Way of Jesus, thoughts and feelings accompany action. It is the act of reaching out that demonstrates your faith. Those who act out of revenge or resentment get back the fruit of unhappiness and despair. Jesus understood that the Law of Attraction mirrored the Law of Consequence. You cannot continue a thought process that is filled with negativity and expect anything in return that isn't negative.

The teachings of Jesus are not always seen as a force for good. There are those who are adamant that the way of Jesus comes across as another positive thinking program that doesn't confront the real issues people need to address. The nay-sayers are convinced that the Law of Attraction sends a false message that results in failure and fear.

There are crimes against humanity so horrific no one can forget them and thus we all remember the pain and tragedy. This memory is not exclusive. It plays within all of humanity's subconscious memory, reinforcing our collective sense of fear and anticipation. Many of those who suffer and survive make a pack that they will never allow such a calamity to happen again.

They might not have identified themselves as victims, but they were never again going to allow themselves to become victims. Something within them examined their outcomes, calculated their risks, studied their emotional history and prepared to defend their lives.

Others, however, choose not to calculate the risks but instead work to end the memories that would objectify others as enemies and/or create violent internal triggers.

"You'll know who they are by what they produce."

Jesus did not prepare to meet the enemy; he prepared to love the enemy. You cannot learn to love your enemy if you're motivated by a worldly memory of fear and danger. To love your enemies you must become motivated by a deep personal connection with a Divine nature that is everywhere.

Remember, we're all connected to the same memory. The fight or flight rule is still a part of our *lizard* brain and is one of the most automatic reactions we have. This reaction has no limitation when it comes to location, race, gender, or tribe. Jesus knew that people could heal their memory by taking the action love dictates: forgiveness.

Number Nine – Nothing can Change Until you Forgive

"...forgive, and you'll be forgiven." Luke 6:37

Spiritual evolution depends on your ability to forgive yourself and others. Think of all the grudges in this world and how much energy they have transformed into hate and war. This is why you cannot allow yourself to live in the toxic nature of thoughts and feelings that create repeated patterns. Forgiveness is a trait exclusive to humans. Our ability to forgive distinguishes us from other species and allows us to expand our scope and extend our range of proactive behavior. As our repertoire of wisdom increases, conflict disappears.

The Law of Attraction works with what you're still angry about or unhappy with. The thoughts and feelings generated by these emotions are destructive and debilitating. Pay attention to what you must forgive, first in yourself and then in the ideas you hold of others.

Put something more in your toolbox than the hammer of discontent. Every night before you go to sleep, consider making two lists. One list of what you think went wrong and another list of what you think went right that day. First, work with the list of what went wrong by visualizing what it would have felt like if things went right. Second, work with the list of what went right and imagine more of that happening in your life. Do this until you can feel the feeling that defines the meaning of living a life in right action — gratitude made real. Once the Universe hears the heart-felt thank you, it unleashes a vast affirmative power that validates and authorizes an even greater good.

Number Ten – Don't Forget the Real Nature of God

"It's like a mustard seed. (It's) the smallest of all seeds, but when it falls on prepared soil, it produces a large plant and becomes a shelter for birds of the sky." Thomas 20:2

A mustard seed is almost invisible to the eye. Yet it grows into a huge bush. So too, the nature of the Law of Attraction remains invisible to the eye. Yet it grows your life into a complex and multi-dimensional experience.

Most people suffer because their complexities put them into a hypnotic state. This is the meaning of being *self-absorbed*. I see many people wandering from circumstance to circumstance, lost in a sea of self-doubt and self-abuse, strangled in their own tangled webs of misfortune. God did not ordain their self-imposed suffering.

These are the stories of the millions of people whose testimony bears witness to what happens when people remember that they are the Spirit of God individualized. The Way of Jesus breaks the hypnotic grip of sin, shame, and guilt. It frees the soul to find the way of love.

When people learn the lessons of the heart, they regain the sight and right of their creation, to live a life of joy, peace, and love.

"Lord, make me an instrument of thy peace. Where there is hatred, let me sow love..."
—Francis of Assisi

Chapter 3
Jesus and the Great Prayer

My Introduction to the Lord's Prayer

In my childhood, I went to bed and said my prayers. I remember Dad at my bedside, the two of us saying the Lord's Prayer aloud. I'm grateful my parents never instilled any fear of God in me or tried to program me into some extreme type of belief that saw me separate from God, unloved or unlovable, afraid to live and be myself. I recall the first version of the Lord's Prayer I learned:

> *Our Father, which art in Heaven*
> *Hallowed be Thy name*

Thy kingdom come, thy will be done
On earth as it is Heaven.
Give us this day, our daily bread
And forgive us our debts, as we forgive our debtors.
And lead us not into temptation, but deliver us
from evil.
For Thine is the kingdom, and the power, and the
glory, forever and ever. Amen

This is a popular version of this great prayer that many still say and sing today.

However, there is another version said to be the original way Jesus spoke this ancient prayer in Aramaic.

Our Father who (is) in Heaven
Holy be your name
Let come your kingdom,
Let be your desire (will)
Even as in Heaven, so on earth
Give us bread for our needs from day to day

Forgive us our offenses, even as was also
forgiven our offenders
And let not us enter into temptation, but part us
from (error) evil
Because yours are kingdom and power and glory
(song)

From ages through ages, sealed in trust, faith and truth.

Holy Be your Name

I never understood "Hallowed be thy name" until I realized that name and nature are the same. When Saul went through his transformation on the road to Damascus, his name changed to Paul. In a similar way, Abram's name changed to Abraham and his wife from Sari to Sarah.

When you decide to be yourself; your true nature and character emerges. You are transformed in the twinkling of an eye. *"Holy be your nature."* When instantaneous transformation happens, it astonishes everyone. Why?

When wisdom taps into the universal consciousness and it becomes available everything changes. Jesus knew why people felt stuck and confined and he knew what would free them: a change in their nature.

To change your nature, you must change what you think. Thought is the key and feelings are the doorway. Too many people have locked themselves up in a prison of unholy thoughts. No wonder they keep getting rejected and into more debt. They can't think of anything but their condition of lack and limitation.

Let Come Your Kingdom

Emerson said we must get our bloated nothingness out of the way.

If you really want the life God created you to live, you must stop trying to create it yourself. Instead, form a partnership with God and then *"Let come your kingdom."*

In my ministry, I tell people, "The Spirit Knows and the Law Obeys." Buddha says, "All that we are is a result of what we have thought."

My kingdom, the life God created me to live, is right now ready to be lived. So why is there resistance?

People change when they accept responsibility for how they think. Prayer will not change the way you think unless you let it. This great prayer starts by recognizing the universal mind, seeing it as the Holy nature of all life. Then it commands this goodness to move and to manifest by means of this life you were given to live. This is the feeling of having a life, not thinking about having a life.

When you become receptive, you pay attention to an inner truth far more real than any current experience.

Let be your desire(will), even as in Heaven, so on earth

Once in tune with the Universal Life Force, your desires become the commands that animate everything necessary for your complete manifestation.

The Law of Attraction doesn't work from the surface of who you are. It works from what you are at the deepest part of your being.

Until you go deeper, you get what you expect, not what you want. To change your expectation, you must know the difference between expectation and expectancy. Expectation blocks the way of life because it stays stuck in conditions and conclusions of the past. Expectancy opens the door for a greater life because expectancy believes that no matter how bad things may be going, something good is emerging.

Give us Bread for Our Needs from Day to Day

Aren't you glad life happens only one day at a time?

Jesus asked for his life one day at a time. He knew that people were off living in the future, scared to death of what might happen. Or they were off living in the past, fearful of what might catch up with them

51

and destroy the life they were trying to create. When you live in fear locked in an emotional prison of "have-nots" you have little or no sense of gratitude.

Jesus visualized his good today, his food today, his life today. See yourself today having all that you desire. Build up in mind a mental image equivalent to what you want.

Bread is a universal word. It means anything that sustains and nurtures your presence. Gratitude and bread will nurture your life and sustain your receptivity. Live in the now, one moment at a time, dedicated to peaceful thoughts and inspired intentions.

Forgive Us our Offenses, Even as We Also Have Forgiven our Offender

We only get what we believe and feel at the deepest core of our being. Forgiveness begins with yourself. Live in the history of your guilt or shame and your biography stops turning the pages of your life. The script stops evolving and you get stuck in a chapter of pain and remorse that repeats like a broken record until you forgive yourself.

Free yourself from your offenses. Surrender yourself to a power capable of absorbing those offenses into the timelessness of Spirit's Infinite Presence. Sit still and declare God's Presence as your presence now. Declare your life forgiven and that you are free to move into a greater expression of love. Let peace be your guide and joy your companion. Let these self-defining principles identify your new life and write your new biography. If you have felt offended, release any and all energy you have about being slighted. There is no other power or time more important than this moment. Live in the moment, not for it.

And Let Not Us Enter into Temptation, but Part Us from (error) Evil

Lisa Nichols, a noted New Thought Speaker, says, "…things that aren't currently working the way you want them to work, don't spend your energy faulting or complaining. Embrace everything that you want so you can get more of it."

Every day your ego tempts you to judge and compare. The ego is forever trying to find something better than what it has. It judges others to justify feelings of rejection or unhappiness. It compares everything to find something wrong that it can fix.

The only temptation is separation. We are tempted to believe we are separate from God. We isolate ourselves by failing to recognize we have the power to change our minds. We walk around in a state of ignorance wishing things would get better or change into a different reality. But things do not change and reality keeps repeating itself.

When separated from the Divine; we fall into a severe lack of appreciation and gratitude; we have no respect for ourselves or others; we see, feel, and know only error (evil).

Love casts out fear and illumines our way through the darkness by becoming the understanding that reconnects us with the Divine.

Because yours are kingdom and power and glory (song)

Jesus ends his great prayer by reminding himself that his life and the power to live it in all its glory awaits his recognition. God created each of us to live a life of authority, not resignation. Most of the world is running away from itself seeking relief instead of healing, trying to find peace instead of being peaceful, looking for the right place instead of knowing they're already in their right place.

To find the truth you must be willing to receive a greater good. To receive a greater good you must visualize what good looks and feels like. It's like a kingdom where you rule, have power, and experience one glory after another. This is the reality of your life and it's ready for you right now. Will you claim it? Or will you be tempted to abandon your potential and live only half a life?

When I go to visit someone in the hospital, I don't go to visit the disease. I go to see the person. I go to see and validate their authority. I go to change my mind so I can see them whole and complete. I don't want to talk about their disease; I want to talk about living free from any limitation or sense of lack.

I have a good friend of mine, Patty Parillo, who had ALS, commonly known as Lou Gehrig's disease. She discovered she had it eight weeks after her husband Tony died of cancer. The doctors told Patty she had two years to live. She lived six.

Her body had the condition, not her. She refused to let anything limit her happiness, peace of mind, or ability to reach out and help others. In other words, she would not be led into temptation. Instead, she prayed and enjoyed every moment of the life given to her to live.

When she finally passed, my wife laid next to her and sang Irish lullabies as she peacefully made her transition.

"It's not what you look at that matter it's what you see."
— Henry David Thoreau

Chapter 4
Seven Keys to Unlocking Your Life

One - Look Only at What You Want

"Never look at that which you do not wish to experience."
Dr. Ernest Holmes, *The Science of Mind*

The Way of Jesus says reality is a mental experience. The creative nature of God can make an acorn or a planet and doesn't know the difference between a million dollars and a penny.

However, we do.

The Law of Attraction creates for each person anything that person wants in accord with his or her faith, belief and acceptance. The Law of Attraction cannot create what you want for another person unless that person asks you to pray for him or her. However, that person must be receptive to the change you are praying for; and even then, your prayer must include the idea of *this or something better*. When you speak your word for another person, you are speaking into God's presence convinced and certain that your word carries the authority of your faith.

For those who keep demonstrating the same problems, you are still fixed to the image of what you do not wish to experience.

To unlock your potential, you must penetrate the illusion, the false evidence that's appearing real, and imagine a new life. A great revelation awaits your discovery the moment you clearly identify what you want and stay focused on it. It's like Aretha Franklin singing over and over just to you: *What you want, baby, I got it!*

Your good awaits you and the key to unlocking your life rests in your ability to visualize your dreams manifesting and experience the feeling of already having what you want NOW!

Your connection with the Divine clarifies what you know. God creates your life, animating your highest thoughts of being alive. This makes you irresistible and attracts the people, conditions, and circumstances best suited to fulfill your vision.

What if your vision remains undeveloped? What if your relationship with the Divine does not exist? What if you have no sense of your own potential? What if you do not trust the life you have been given to live?

I remember the first 10 weeks of my first ministry. I had resigned my teaching position in California, moved to Florida and assumed the position as Senior Minister for a 125-member church with their own building. This was exciting stuff, and I was confident for a while. Then six weeks into my ministry one of my board members decided I did not fit his idea of a minister so he left the church. Devastated, I called my sponsor, Rev. Roy Graves and I remember at some point in our conversation I said, "Roy, I'm going through hell and I don't know what to do."

I never forgot his retort, "Jim, when you are going through hell, don't stop. Keep doing your job and those folks who identify with you will stay and the ones who don't will go. Your hell is in your imagination focused on the expectation that everyone will love you." Roy ended our conversation and did an affirmative prayer for the church and me. I hung up and immediately got busy doing my work, and in a short time I walked out of my hell and into a consciousness free from fear and uncertainty.

Wake up, unlock the door, your true self reveals your purpose and reason for being alive. Sense your presence and see yourself in a much larger context. Your horizon expands and you see past the pretense of achievement. Your acceptance and confidence beget a feeling of vulnerability and peace. You know you are one with all life. You see it, you find it, you feel it, you are what you're looking for.

Jesus lived the example of, *"love your enemies and do good."* This Divine Guidance, once aligned with your inner presence of God, will give direction to the Law of Attraction and activate its energy. This is how reality comes into form.

Money is energy in form. We even define the symbols of money by assigning value to pieces of paper: one, five, ten, twenty and so on.

What about you? Have you assigned value to your life?

How do you value your life and the lives of those around you? When you look at yourself or another with a diminished sense of value; you take energy away from form and limit your possibilities. Your sense of worth is reflected in what you feel and think. The higher or more spiritual your thoughts and feelings, the greater reflection of God. You may not be what you want, but sooner or later you will see your life in the result of what you accept, think and feel.

Want a better life? Accept it each day. Allow yourself to receive more. Don't be concerned with what the world thinks you are worth. Self-worth is not determined by the world unless you accept the world's opinion of who you are and what you're worth. Assign value to your life. Focus on an image of what that value means. Allow more good to move by means of what you think and how you feel.

Free yourself from limitation. Accept more good today than you had yesterday. Receive your good with appreciation and gratitude. This creates momentum to receive even more good into your life.

Two – Never Limit Your View of Life

"The possibility of life is inherent within the capacity to imagine what life is, backed by the power to produce the imagery, or Divine Imagination."
Dr. Ernest Holmes, *The Science of Mind*

For too long, humanity has believed that life is a process of success and failure, good and bad, right and wrong. Life does not have to be experienced this way! Successful people succeed because they see themselves as successful. They watch their thoughts with care and dismiss the negative as unreal.

Unsuccessful people tend to focus on one thing—what it feels like to be unsuccessful. Unhappy and unsuccessful people often think about themselves in the dark and they wonder if there is a way out.

"The light of the body is the eye: therefore, when your eye is single, your whole body also is full of light; but when your eye is evil, your body also is full of darkness. Take heed therefore that the light which is in you be not darkness." Luke 11:34, 35

Unsuccessful people need to be disillusioned. I've often told my congregation that we need to take the unhappy people out behind the wood shed and pray the unhappiness out them. This is not a beating, but a rejoicing. Once you tell God what you want and have joyfully accepted it as yours for the asking, you've remove the barriers to your good. But will you do this?

It may look like we're dealing with an intangible concept, but the principle that creates life in accord with what you believe is as real as your big toe. The power to create is what keeps each person upright and moving forward. Does your point of view limit your outcome? Your results depend on how you define what's possible. This is the job of your imagination.

Walt Disney, the greatest proponent of the imagination, called what he did Imagineering. The process of conception and creation excites the senses. I know that the dream may seem like an illusion, but only because you have not accepted it for yourself. Instead, you have used time and space to distance yourself from what you really want, and the bigger the gap, the darker the path. Separation and sin are the same.

Jesus kept telling everyone he healed, *"Your faith has made you whole."* At what point in your life will you let go of having faith in the wrong things and start to practice a life of constructive beliefs? The Way of Jesus works because those who are willing to practice are set free.

Here's something you can practice saying aloud:

Today I remember my source and trust that God knows what God is doing by means of me. Every new thought is filled with a greater feeling for life. Every moment presents another possibility for a spiritual transaction. Every day is a blessing. I expect the good! And I am open to receiving it into my life with gratitude.

Three – Never Compromise

"In demonstrating over conditions, the only inquiries we need to make are: 'Do the things we want lend themselves to a constructive program? Do they express a more abundant life, rob no one, create no delusion, and express a greater degree of livingness?'"
Dr. Ernest Holmes, *The Science of Mind*

Whatever the Law of Attraction does for you it must do through you. Jesus knew that he did not do the work himself—the authority within him did the work. The Way of Jesus redirects you back to your own thinking. You can't make progress until you change your mind and keep it changed. The inner part of your thoughts fueled by your feelings creates the outer experience. You are, on the surface, the sum total of your memorized emotional and intellectual reactions.

When Jesus said that you should first love God with all your heart, mind, and soul and then love your neighbor as yourself, he was explaining how the Law defines your life.

But why love God first? Why not love what you want and then love God?

Not everything you want will be for your highest good. Jesus said to focus on your love of God first. That way, you can be assured that you will think constructively and with a greater degree of lovingness. Gradually you will see that abundance lives everywhere and the supply is unlimited. You will cease to compromise and become the love of God in action.

Four – Place No Limit on Principle

"The words which you speak would be just as powerful as the word which Jesus spoke, if you knew your word was the Law whereunto it was sent, but you must KNOW this WITHIN and not merely accept it with your intellect."
Dr. Ernest Holmes, *The Science of Mind*

The Law of Attraction defines itself as God in everything. This truth sets you free and energizes everything you were created to experience. Know it on the inside and have confidence in your ability to SPEAK YOUR WORD FOR YOUR HIGHEST GOOD.

I suggest you write down your dreams and keep a gratitude journal. Write your dreams onto paper. Then speak your word. This conscious act of paying attention to what matters keeps you connected to the source.

Be careful, though, not to describe your dream by saying what you don't want. Develop an affirmative voice and learn how to use this voice to keep verbalizing your dream.

The self-defining nature of your life awaits this voice and treats it like a command. It affects every cell in your body and lights up your face with a look of joy, expectancy, and hope. It makes you irresistible to your good. Gone are the unholy thoughts of limitation and lack. Erased are the memories of a diminished capacity to receive. Canceled is anything unlike your desire. The stronger the message, the more affirmative the idea, the more life giving the words, the more will be attracted to you. It's like a light that illuminates the truth revealing what needs to happen, manifest, or be seen.

I had a pastor friend of mine who bought a piece of property to build a church. The property, part of an estate sale, required him to go to court to submit his bid. Many people wanted that property but he wanted it more, so he made the highest bid and promised to make a substantial down payment within ten business days. He did this even though he did not have the down payment, however he did know the source from whence it would come; and because his mind was one with God's mind, it was a done deal. In other words, he knew the down payment already existed in his mind. He visualized and held true to what he wanted and within a few days he had it.

The Law of Attraction responds to affirmative thoughts and feelings. Write your dreams on paper. Declare them present and available. Unlock the energy they contain and free them to manifest.

Five – The Law of Attraction Is a Mental Practice

"... (a) philosophy... of healing is based upon the conception that we are living in a universe of Intelligence – a spiritual Universe; that thoughts are things, that definite states of consciousness...tend to reproduce themselves in form."
Dr. Ernest Holmes, *The Science of Mind*

The Way of Jesus is works with light, not darkness. It does this because "it overcomes the darkness; not by combating darkness, but by being exactly what it is: LIGHT. *And the light shineth in the darkness; and the darkness comprehended it not.*" It takes a strong desire to change your mind and turn away from the conditions and circumstances you unconsciously focus on.

Why is it so difficult to stay focused on the good?

Goodness, the reality of God, does not exist in the reality most people focus on in the world. Jesus knew this and stated it by saying, *"Whoever tries to hang on to life will forfeit it, but whoever forfeits life will preserve it." Luke 17:33.* This statement doesn't make sense until you understand Jesus' meaning: Life is a changing dynamic in a Changeless Reality. You lose what you hate by giving up what you love. The Law of Attraction is impersonal. It creates whatever you embody. And to love something means you're

67

willing to set it free. This is a mental practice that requires discipline and consistency.

But why give up what you love?

Love, a spiritual principle and a changeless reality, seeks to be expressed by those willing to experience growth and expansion. People, however, grow in an inconsistent manner because they're confused about what they love and want for themselves. Most people define their life by what makes them unhappy.

This is where LIGHT is so important. The Way of Jesus says go back and rethink your desires and focus on visualizing yourself as already successful. Jesus says give up what you hate and use your love as a light to convert your thoughts into feelings of love, care, and compassion. Another way of saying this is, "Unlock your love and let it loose into the world so all may see the benefit of your God-given life."

Six – Turn Entirely from the Condition

"The reason you have difficulty in throwing off some weakness of character – while believing in Spirit implicitly and having faith that you are going to overcome your limitation – is because you have not induced the necessary images in mind."
Dr. Ernest Holmes, *The Science of Mind*

You can't overcome trouble by looking at it, expecting it to go away. If you're serious about changing your life and unlocking your magnificence you must TURN AWAY FROM TROUBLE. But turning away from the condition is hard because we tend to put the emphasis on the feeling of either making the error, or worse, being the error. The way to initiate change is to see the experience of trouble as nothing more than an opinion of what is happening. If you focus on the feeling of your weakness, you keep the image of it before you. If you focus on the feeling of what you want, your image can translate the feeling nature into the physiology of what it means to have it now.

Language is a mental experience that literally fires the connections in the brain, creating images and symbols of what it wants. This immediately activates a search for a corresponding experience and starts drawing you closer and closer to the reality of what you imagine life to be. On this journey, we may pass through what appears to be destructive conditions, but if we can let the disturbances pass, we will have found the Way of Jesus. An idea popular in Jesus' time: *judge not according to appearance, but righteous judgment*, a short lesson with a powerful logic that can change your mind and take you to a way of living that you've never known before.

The ego looks for trouble and if it can't find any, it manufactures trouble. To keep your ego in check you must turn away from the thoughts that correspond to your feelings of fault, shame and blame. You must step away from the FOG of Fear, Obligation, and Guilt and enter into a new vision. And it doesn't matter how compelling the trouble may be, STEP AWAY FROM YOUR TROUBLE AND OPEN A NEW DOORWAY OF POSITIVE POTENTIAL!

Seven – The Universe Is Perfect

"...the student of Truth will maintain that he or she lives in a Perfect Universe and among people potentially perfect. He or she will regulate his or her thinking to meet this necessity and will refuse to believe in its opposite."
Dr. Ernest Holmes, *The Science of Mind*

I have always believed in the perfection of God. The Universe is the perfect out-picturing of a whole and complete idea. If God is perfect, then God's creation must also be perfect. It is impossible for me to conclude that a perfect power would create an imperfect creation. The idea of human imperfection is strictly a human idea created by a misuse of one's power to create. The Way of Jesus insists that thoughts and feelings are the key to unlocking the infinite goodness of life. The reason that people have not created their dream is because they keep staring at the nightmare, the trouble, the problem, the limitation.

Your life has brought you to this moment to create something greater than you've ever known or experienced before. If you are feeling overwhelmed by your current reality, stop everything you're thinking, doing, or knowing, and right now turn and answer this question: If age, money, time, experience, status, health, or position is no object, what do I want? As Neale Donald Walsh says, "Life is a blackboard waiting to be filled in."

"...a house divided against a house falls." Luke 11:18 Don't let your dreams and desires become separate from your actions. Keep the image and feeling of the dream alive and well by seeing yourself having what you want. Keep thinking, what would it feel like to have my dream come true? How would my life change? The only way to draw your good to you is to draw it through you. The Way of Jesus lives within and is ready right now to manifest your life if you will give it a way to work through you.

The Universe is something you can trust. It created you to manifest its treasure. But it can only measure the good based upon your measure of the treasure. If the treasure within remains hidden by your thoughts, would you clear away the obstruction? Would you open your heart so the energy of your life could energize your world and give you the experience of a life you yearn to live but are afraid to? If you want happiness you must learn to trust the life you've been given to live. *"Hear, Israel, the Lord your God is one Lord, and you are to love God with all your heart and all your soul and all your mind and with all your energy." Mark 12: 29*

"What lies behind us and what lies ahead of us are tiny matters compared to what lives within us."
—Henry David Thoreau

Chapter 5
The Law of Attraction

The Mystery

The Way of Jesus looks like a mystery; it says *life is an inner experience.* No matter what happens on the outside, your experience is always internal.

What happens to you is not as important as what happens inside you, and what happens inside is governed by your thoughts, feelings, memories, habits, external stimuli, and your dreams.

To solve the mystery, you must remember:

It's not what happened to you that matters, it's what you think happened to you.

One of the two great discoveries of life, *thoughts become things* and *memories tend to return as experience.* Your memory of how life changes obscures your view. This mystery causes few to look within for the answers to what they think, feel or experience. Attention, drawn outwards, compels you to consider the condition as the source of the thought that created your experience. Two people can look at the same object and have two different experiences. It all depends on the emotions and memories stimulated by their point of view.

Nobody remembers the facts of their history as much as they remember how an experience made them feel. Napoleon said, "History is a fable agreed upon." Emerson said, "There is no history, only biography." Jesus is reported to have said,

"Those who love life lose it, but those who hate life in this world will preserve (and mistake) it for unending, real life." John 12: 25

You preserve what you hate and you lose what you love? The Way of Jesus insists that *what you focus on you create*. Life and love are moveable feasts, dynamic and creative expressions that change as you grow and mature.

People who hate their jobs, relationships, or conditions seem to live in an unending experience of disappointment and unhappiness. They try to preserve history. They try to keep something alive that should have changed a long time ago.

Jesus came from a family of carpenters, but there is no report that he used that trade to support himself. Instead, he ate the best food, stayed with the wealthiest people, road the Cadillac of the day, a donkey, and wore a seamless robe. He lived his life as a biography, letting each day be a new page in which he did his work, lived his life, and made his contribution. He lived by the Law of Attraction.

The Twinkling of an Eye

You have a life ready to be lived. If you really want a more meaningful life, you must learn to quiet your mind and allow the internal presence of God to guide your actions and transform your experience. When you are in a trance caused by a condition, reality escapes your observance. Conditions hypnotize and trap you in circumstances that need a wake-up call.

Learn this difficult truth: *you are always in your right place and nature is calling you to wake up*. The moment you wake up, you become aware of your identity and find yourself in a world of plenty. This all happens in the twinkling of an eye, and brings you to a place where abundance, harmony, confidence, Life and Truth eclipse your thoughts of confusion, trouble, problems, and misfortune.

One way to suspend your disbelief is to put it on hold for a few weeks. Dismiss doubt and worry from your thought process. If either one of them rear their ugly head inside your thoughts, turn and terminate. Do not let worry or doubt take root. Instead, start your day with a period of quiet meditation and deliberate thought. In other words, INVOKE THE LAW OF ATTRACTION TO WORK ON YOUR MOST CONSTRUCTIVE THOUGHTS.

You can't turn off your thinking. Instead, you must direct it mentally to embody thoughts about a new life. At first, this new life may seem like a dream, but insist your mind accept it as something already accomplished (at least for two-weeks). Let this way of thinking become your inner affirmation...*life is now rushing to fulfill my highest desire*.

Dismiss any temptation to question your desire or limit its full and complete manifestation. This is what we call in philosophy *creating a mental atmosphere.* The mind cannot tell the difference between what you believe and what you perceive. If you keep looking at poverty, lack, unhappiness, or limitation, you will start to think about these things and manifest their experience.

You must turn away from these thoughts and images and immediately replace them with healthy, whole, complete ideas. This is an exercise designed to TRAIN YOUR MIND HOW TO THINK.

Where Do I Start

What are you looking at? What are you feeling?

Is it good, fulfilling, and creative?

If not, stop looking at it. Imagine what creation feels like.

This is not rocket science; it's work. For too long you've been listening to reports of lack, pain, and suffering. Stop studying counterproductive ideas. Start studying productive thoughts. Put only good stuff in and great stuff will happen.

If despair wants your attention, REFUSE! Say aloud, *"Despair, you are not welcome here, but my good is. I now see the goodness of all that I desire manifesting in the flesh, right before my eyes. Thank you, God, for giving me so many blessings."*

Your life has its origin in the law. Life takes form by converting the attention of your thoughts and feelings into life experience. What you think and feel matters.

Yesterday I played golf with a friend of mine and his game did not go well. He struggled with his timing and couldn't hit the ball. I asked, "Are you having a hard time concentrating?"

He said, "I feel *punky*, like I'm overloaded processing something."

"All is good," I said. "You are processing something, just let it move through you. Tell yourself to focus on the game."

Immediately, he smiled, nodded and relaxed. The tension in his face disappeared and his game improved. In the twinkling of an eye, he transformed his life by redirecting his thought to a more productive idea.

Limitation, lack or death did not fascinate or impress Jesus, even though it impresses the Christian community! Suffer and re-live the experience of his death and you might miss the point of his life, that there is no death.

The Way of Jesus does not correct your mistakes. It corrects your point of view. Jesus walked through the barriers of pain, suffering, and limitation to prove they were not the reason you live. Jesus, the Rabbi, the teacher, healer, and myth buster sought to redirect our minds and show us the way of love, compassion, and forgiveness.

Jesus' life portrayed the example, not the exception. He showed us the Way of peace. Many say Jesus died for our sins (mistakes). I believe he lived to prove there is no death and that our Creator intended for all of us to have the experience of heaven on earth. To use an old sailing term, we had to come about to bring it about. We have to steer a new course, not away from tradition, but towards the timeless and infinite life God intends us to live.

The Law of Attraction models the Way of Jesus, the Way of Peace, and the Way of Love, which brings us to an important question.

Who's in Control and What Are You In Control Of?

Everything comes into your life based on the activity of your thought. Nothing outside of you controls the way you think unless you let it. Your experience of the world changes the moment you regain control of how you think. No one can free you from your unhappiness but you. You are only limited because you do not know this truth.

Tell people their experience of life rests in the way they think and they want to argue. They review their conditions and — in vivid detail — tell you their stories of rejection, failure, and effort. They're firmly convinced that something outside of themselves controls their existence. The Way of Jesus improves the way you think and feel because it sidesteps your story and changes your mind about who you are and the power you possess.

It's a struggle to accept responsibility for disappointments and unhappiness without feelings of guilt, shame, or blame. It's a struggle to imagine the absence of those feelings. You might be able to think a new thought, but that doesn't change your old negative emotional memory. THIS IS A COMMON PROBLEM WITH THE LAW OF ATTRACTION.

The recurring dominant thought patterns sound something like this:

I want to believe, but I can't force myself to change the way I feel. My sense of betrayal, resentment, anger, and need to control the outcome is too strong.

The culprit here is EMOTIONAL MEMORY. How can you sidestep memory?

Your emotional memory steers your life in one direction and you can't make it change direction by wishing your life, like a car, would go somewhere else. You must deliberately steer your attention to where you want your life to go. Emotional memory, like the ultimate back seat driver, harasses you, blames you, infuriates you and manipulates you to stay on the same course of unhappiness because it promises you a predictable result, a steady diet of failure with an occasional success.

The Way of Jesus sidesteps the back-seat driver and remains in control to stay the course of understanding that brings heaven on earth. Guilt, shame and fear will not take you where you want to go.

Whatever you reflect into Mind tends to take form. STOP LOOKING AT AND HEADING IN THE DIRECTION OF LIMITATION! You're only interested because you haven't given your mind something else to think about that's more intellectually powerful or emotionally rewarding than your current thoughts and feelings. What you need is a way to think that can return you to the truth and set you free.

Prayer Is the Key to Happiness

People see prayer as a sort of begging Jesus or begging God to change the outcome of your life. How many times have you thought God would intervene if you would do something for God? God doesn't bargain. God fulfills.

God's not even aware that you have a problem. This is not widely known. It is more traditional to think that God is watching you, judging you, and estimating your worth.

How do you pray to such a God? Do you hope to change God's mind about you?

This is not a God of love. This is a God of retribution made in the image of mankind.

Defining God is the key. The Way of Jesus holds that God is the Law of Attraction in action as your most dominant thoughts and feelings. Jesus taught the same. *"There is nothing veiled that won't be unveiled, or hidden that won't be made known." Luke 12:2*

YOU CAN'T HIDE FROM THE CONSEQUENCES OF YOUR THOUGHTS AND FEELINGS.

The first step in any prayer is the recognition that you're working with *pure intelligence and that when you pray, you act intelligent.* God is your creator and ally, a loving Presence that knows you as WHOLE, PERFECT, AND COMPLETE. Why would God create you and then know you as imperfect, incomplete, and incompetent?

Only your mind can perceive yourself this way!

No wonder fear is rampant. The collective experience of humanity has memorized its sense of isolation. The Way of Jesus frees people from their separation by revealing a truth always known, but seldom applied: You are in God and God is in you.

Prayer is the application of the Law of Attraction. The Way of Jesus awakens the sleeping magnificence within and helps humanity redirect the way it thinks and feels.

A Simple Way to Pray

The American Sign Language for God is to place the palm of the right hand perpendicular to your body and in front of the heart. Bring your hand to this position in a gentle sweeping motion while consciously inhaling and then exhaling. Hold the hand in position until all your air is expelled and then wait for God to take the next breath—don't try to hold your breath, just wait...your body will take it for you.

In Latin, the word for spirit and breath is the same: *Spiritus*. In Eastern spirituality, the breath is called *Prana* and considered the same as Spirit.

Many times, the human mind is just too manic to be brought into right relationship with God and made still by just thinking. To apply the Way of Jesus you need a way to put yourself in right relationship with God, focused and calm.

The simplest way to pray is to combine breath and physical movement—focusing the Spirit and the mind into a state of *being*. As you consciously take the first breath and move your hand into position, consciously expelling the air; you're mental and physical nature aligns with the moment and time disappears. This is not hard to do and it works every time.

I developed this method of prayer because many people tell me they can't, on command, still their minds and calm their thinking. I call this approach *The Sacred Language of Dimensional Prayer.* There are twelve movements and they constitute a method that can and does focus the mind and open it to receive whatever the Divine needs to communicate to guide and direct your life.

I offer the first step in this approach because it is something you can do that will bring you to a state of peace and stillness. If you commit to staying still for a minimum of three breaths, you will experience ONENESS (a sense of connectedness).

This one-step can accomplish the first goal of prayer, which is to align your being with God's presence, feeling connected, calm and conscious. Next, focus on a sacred defining principle to provide your mind with a concept from which life can be conceived.

These principles are also called verities or basic truths. They include: Life, Love, Light, Beauty, Peace, Joy, and Truth. To simplify, pick one or defer to the most popular, Love.

A principle is something that can define thoughts, feelings, and desires. For instance, if you pick Peace, take a breath, expel the air, and bring your hand in front of your heart. As you breathe, imagine that every breath you take is an act of Peace.

It is important not to try to define the principle but to let the principle define you. Visualize the principle acting by means of you in how you think, behave, feel, and react. See the idea of the principle coming to life as your life.

Once centered on the principle see the principle acting by means of you manifesting and attracting to you all that is necessary for your highest and greatest good.

To review this simple method:

1. Consciously inhale, bringing your hand in front of your heart. While exhaling the air, focus on the hand as if it were the Principle Itself.

2. As you exhale, wait and allow God to take the next three breaths. Focus on your hand as a symbolic representation of the Principle.

3. Imagine your life fulfilled and complete.

4. Give thanks for all your blessings.

5. Release your word and let God work by means of you, guiding, directing and inspiring your feelings, thoughts and deeds.

Be the Blessing You Want

Your Spirit, soul and body are in complete harmony with the inner actor, medium, and result. Your life is a seamless experience of faith, belief and acceptance. Life may look like it's divided, but it's not. There is only One Power and It performs in accord with your word. Once you see the blessing that God has bestowed through the Law of Attraction and you accept responsibility for what you think, how you feel and the way you act, you will have better, higher and more loving thoughts.

As Dr. Ernest Holmes wrote, "They don't punish the math teacher because he or she didn't get the right answer," and God doesn't punish you because you didn't know the truth. But you can suffer from such ignorance until you finally set life free to become the blessing you want to see.

Gandhi said, "Be the change you want to see." The Law of Attraction provides the venue. All we need do is choose from the menu of Love, Life, and Light.

"What you're supposed to do when you don't like a thing is change it. If you can't change it, change the way you think about it."
—Maya Angelou

Chapter 6
Forgiveness and Gratitude

The Truth About Forgiveness

The Western model for traditional religion and medicine both suffer from the same limitation, dominator thinking. There is a reason for this.

Picture the alpha-dog phenomena. Wherever two or more dogs are gathered, one dog must be in charge. This is not by accident; it's evolution. Species that interact survive by having the strongest of its members lead and mate. This would seem to ensure that a significant number of offspring will inherit the sturdiest genetic codes based on the concept of the survival of the fittest.

This, however, is not the Way of Jesus. Darwin never talked about the success of a species as *survival of the fittest*. What he wrote sounded more like those who cooperate with each other will live where others die.

Traditional academic religion and medicine, however, have been fighting for the alpha position for hundreds of years. The problematic nature of science in competition with the supernatural is a house divided against itself. The public is caught in the intellectual and emotional crossfire that tests loyalty, faith, and doctrine in an invisible civil war whose wounds are seen in the disenfranchised and powerless feelings of those who want to be healed, not codependent upon drugs, diagnosis, or doctrine.

This is also a primary problem when it comes to forgiveness.

The dominator is genetically cued in the human experience; the forgiver is not. The one who sees cooperation as more important than competition did not evolve to this position; he or she invented it. In his book, *Thumbs, Toes, and Tears*, Chip Walter says that research shows that sometimes our state of mind has each of our feet placed in different camps, "The primal one for which we evolved, and the modern one we invented. One shaped by our DNA, the other created by our big brains. Sometimes they seem to be diametrically opposed."

This might be a partial answer to the question: Why is forgiveness so difficult?

It's difficult to forgive some people because, in part, our dominator genes are in a battle for survival, pitting instinct against a doctrine of *should* as in, *"you shouldn't feel this way."* It feels wrong to forgive some people because at the core of our human genetic code it means the death of our species. Some of our aggression is the outcome of a predisposed genetic need to protect descendants. Many are conflicted about forgiveness because it doesn't feel natural.

Jesus knew this on a sacred level that did not come from scientific knowledge. His reasoning came from a different kind of knowledge, an *intuitive awareness*. Each of us is connected to an invisible and infinite supply of ideas that is not known in the world as a practical and pragmatic source of information. Yet, all great invention, art, science, math, poetry, and music came by way of our INTUITION THROUGH OUR IMAGINATION — which is what Einstein alluded to when he said, "Imagination is more important than knowledge."

Imagination and faith are mechanical mental talents we all possess and use. Like the Law of

Attraction, we seldom acknowledge their importance and tend to minimize the role they play in how our lives turn out. But consider this, if my fear-based memory recognizes a behavior or a circumstance as a threat, my mechanical imagination will instantly begin to out-picture the threat and start planning defensive and offensive action. It doesn't matter if the threat is real or *imagined*, if I haven't trained my mind to respond with forgiveness and gratitude, survival will be my only thought, my primal instinct. This is why the first two cause and effect teachings of Jesus are LOVE YOUR ENEMIES and DON'T REACT VIOLENTLY.

In the world of human and genetic terms and conditions, it seems perfectly natural to want to survive and protect. But in universal terms, conditions are not ruled by genetics, science, or politics. Conditions are the byproduct of how we apply or don't apply SPIRITUAL PRINCIPLES. And PRINCIPLES are the way we train and thus define our moral and ethical behavior.

The life of Socrates exemplifies the contradiction of feeling pulled by conditions that resist being peaceful, finding resentment and revenge more appropriate. Socrates, convicted of corrupting the youth of Athens, proved that, while dominance could control outcomes, it would not lead to peace.

Early in his life Socrates trained to be a Sophist, a clever teacher who used logic to trap people and make them look foolish. This did not gain him friends. Instead, Athens labeled him the gadfly because he annoyed those he trapped in his Socratic Method of Questioning.

But like a gadfly, I'm sure Socrates annoyed himself because he repented and changed his mind and began to teach a different path that lead to a new kind of world. Socrates, like Jesus, did not need to dominate or even win an argument. He trained his mind to free people not trap them. The clever mind motivated by guile disguises itself in sheep's clothing waiting to trap the untrained mind and consume its time, space, and assets. Socrates went deep below the surface where the trained mind gathers ideas that change the way we think, behave and live.

Your experience, however, does not depend on conditions; it depends on whether or not you have a TRAINED MIND OR AN UNTRAINED MIND.

The Trained Mind

The untrained mind, fueled by instinct, REACTS. The trained mind, powered by a balance of instinct and intuition, BECOMES PROACTIVE.

Steven Covey, in his watershed book, *Seven Habits of Highly Effective People*, defines the proactive mind as one that is trained to spend more time creating opportunity then dealing with conflicts.

The trained mind must have *authority* to think independent of how it instinctually reacts. The Way of Jesus helps you develop your authority and explains its nature. How you use it to manifest the life you want to live depends upon how you exercise the authority of your word. The Way of Jesus returns people to the power of choice—a choice stolen by fear and limited by doubt. This turns the table on toxic traditions because when people abandon convention for creation, they re-member and re-join their spiritual origin.

The trained mind uses thoughts and feelings to focus attention on vision. The untrained mind repeats itself wondering why it's bored and unfulfilled. The trained mind is busy creating the life it wants by making itself available to the resources rushing to it through the Law of Attraction.

We are surrounded by energy and directed by thoughts and feelings that command energy to take form. Life's mental, emotional, and physical nature remains constructive when we employ a proactive attitude that prepares us to receive.

This is why the placebo effect works. If you are convinced that you're doing something which creates an outcome, it's very likely that you will have that outcome in one form or another. Jesus understood this healing power. The power of faith fuels the activity of what people want and attracts them to the result they are looking for governed by their level of conviction.

This makes gratitude omnipotent. Being thankful is a mental and emotional energy that—without exception—produces positive results. I don't know anyone who suffered, got sick, or struggled with being depressed because of gratitude.

Gratitude and Generosity

"This is why I keep telling you, trust that you will receive everything you pray and ask for, and that's the way it will turn out." Mark 11:24

Jesus discovered the power of faith and imagination as he developed his relationship with God. Jesus lived his life by means of the moral and ethical principles of gratitude and forgiveness. He modeled his behavior based on what he wanted to see in the world, and used his power to imagine life as whole and complete. He applied his faith by training his mind to see the best—loving his enemies and resisting the temptation to react violently. HE DID NOT LIVE FROM THE DESIRE TO SURVIVE; HE LIVED FROM THE DESIRE TO SERVE.

He validated his intuitive-based thoughts through prayer and authorized his vision through faith, a faith he trained to respond, especially when his instincts wanted to retaliate.

The power of the Law of Attraction, always in play, awaits your trust. The consequences for not trusting it are painful and embarrassing. This is why gratitude is so powerful. If you view your debt as something bad or depressing and your payments to that debt are filled with resentment, you'll want to retaliate against something—and it's usually yourself.

Who in their right mind would be thankful when their instincts are telling them that something's wrong or someone's not right? Jesus lived in a trained mind filled with gratitude! Jesus knew the untrained mind would replay the memory of failure and seek to dominate or run.

The Trained Mind versus the Untrained Mind
THE TRAINED MIND
The trained mind will see the opportunity to forgive the failure and seek to heal the habit and feeling of debt.

"Forgive our debts to the extent that we have forgiven those in debt to us." Matthew 6:12

THE UNTRAINED MIND

The untrained mind will go into the darkness of depression and try to explain the memory by assigning blame and shame to all guilty parties then try to remove the blame and shame through a sort of pretend forgiveness that intellectually forgives, but never emotionally forgets.

THE TRAINED MIND

The trained mind will dismiss the darkness and live in the light of expressed gratitude for ALL that it has experienced and accepts that a greater good is now rushing into its experience.

"Take care, then, that the light within you is not darkness. If then your whole body is flooded with light, and no corner of it is darkness, it will be completely illuminated as when a lamp's rays engulf you." Luke 11:35, 36

THE UNTRAINED MIND

The untrained mind will self-medicate through drugs, alcohol, pills, food, work or sex.

THE TRAINED MIND

The trained mind will do what twelve-step programs recommend: a fearless inventory of behavior, and then seek to make amends for that behavior.

"Why do you notice the sliver in your friend's eye, but overlook the timber in your own?" Matthew 7:3-5

THE UNTRAINED MIND

The untrained mind will fear for its loved ones in time of danger, misfortune, addiction, or disease.

THE TRAINED MIND

The trained mind will see fear for what it is, False Evidence Appearing Real, and dismiss the doubt of disbelief and enter into alignment with the universal principles of forgiveness and gratitude and give their imagination something to extol and magnify.

"It's like a mustard seed. (It's) the smallest of all seeds, but when it falls on prepared soil, it produces a large plant and becomes a shelter for birds of the sky." Thomas 20:2

The trained mind is prepared to grow what it consciously plants.

THE UNTRAINED MIND

The untrained mind cannot see the wisdom of gratitude because it responds instinctually to protect its status, property, and/or station.

THE TRAINED MIND

The trained mind is not focused on worldly status or station. It's connected to a universal law of life that is infinite and forever creative. The trained

mind does not seek reward here or hereafter. The trained mind eliminates space and time and lives in the only place the Holy Spirit operates: The Here and Now!

"But love your enemies, and do good, and lend, expecting nothing in return...and you'll be children of the Most High. As you know, he (the universal) is generous to the ungrateful and the wicked. For the standard you apply will be the standard applied to you." Luke 6:35-38

THE UNTRAINED MIND

The untrained mind looks to the world with opinions and reports of the NAYSAYERS for its answers.

THE TRAINED MIND

The trained mind looks within and contemplates the only real authority it knows to be true, universal principle.

"When you pray, go into a room by yourself and shut the door behind you." Matthew 6:5

The trained mind does not work with the opinions or reports of the world. It works within and relies upon universal principles to be the WAY SAYER.

The Doorway

My door is always open. I know you've heard this before, but do you believe it?

The world sees this statement as problematical. If you had a problem and your boss encouraged you to come to him or her with your problems, you would probably resist because you might think that your unimportant problem would just make matters worse.

But what if your boss—your Creator, Source and Supply—couldn't see you with a problem, even if you said you had one? Would you go see the boss?

The doorway to the Divine is blocked by such conundrums, human riddles which Science and Tradition view as *human resource problems* or *other worldly mysteries.* A corporate environment would require negotiation, policy, procedures, and/or rulings. This may be true in the corporate world, but not in the spiritual world.

The doorway to the Divine remains locked by human and worldly perception. The only keys that can open these doors are forgiveness and gratitude. To reach for these keys, you must train yourself to seek progress and opportunity blocked and locked by condition and circumstance. The untrained mind has three keys it uses to pretend it is opening: prediction, control, and analysis. These are the keys of Traditional Science, Traditional Religion, and Traditional Medicine.

The trained mind carries two keys, *forgiveness* and *gratitude*. These keys do not preclude the importance of prediction, control, and/or analysis. On the contrary, forgiveness and gratitude, aligned with a higher power, open the scope and range of perception and enable you to see things the empirical world cannot see. Death is seen as transformation. Fear is cast out by love. Hatred is neutralized by forgiveness, and debt is healed through gratitude and generosity.

If your human mind is yelling at you as you read these simple truths, consider this:

> *"I swear to you, if you have trust and do not doubt...everything you ask for in prayer you'll get if you trust." Matthew 21: 21, 22*

Do you think Jesus aimed his ministry to a few Christians? Jesus, the rabbi, did not know Christians because Christians did not exist.

As I said in my introduction, many serious Jesus scholars are convinced he did not say the words Christians most often quote to justify their religious exclusivity — not even close.

"No one gets left behind, remember?"
—**Mitch Albom**, *The Five People You Meet in Heaven*

Chapter 7
No One Left Behind

The Secular Voice of Change

Religion and science fear change and try to control creation by giving voice to that which labels and estimates what's possible and what's dangerous. The reaction to the Way of Jesus, once it becomes successful, is predictable and consistent with the types of labels and judgments attached to that which threatens the status quo. "Dangerous…" "Warmed-over positive thinking…" "Pseudoscientific, psycho spiritual babble…" Such labels crucify the messenger and suppress the message of faith the Universal Presence gives to humanity.

Traditional religion and science are in the business of manipulating outcomes. They see God in human form, a tangible idol of fame and fortune, and a science of controllable outcomes and predictable diseases we must prepare (or pay) to endure.

Traditional religion and science see all other explanations for people's healings and breakthroughs as coincidental, unpredictable and *dangerously* unreliable.

Controlled by a very specific MODEL OF CAUSE AND EFFECT, the traditional voice of religion and science in the Western world remains set in their ways. Science sees cause in the observation of measurable and repeatable experience. Western religious thought—Judaism, Christianity, and Islam—sees cause as obedience to the rules of a supernatural power defining rewards for those who comply and penalties for those who don't.

In either case, the consequence is clear: FOLLOW THE RULES OR YOU'LL BE LEFT BEHIND. TAKE THE MEDICINE OR YOU WON'T GET BETTER.

Traditional Science and Religion tell stories. In science, the storyteller restricts their comments to what the experiment reveals. In religion, the storyteller is limited to how rules and doctrine apply. Illness can be caused by stress, environment, and/or DNA...sin, fate, and/or God's will. In either discipline the message to humanity is the same: You are limited by the world and only a few will succeed. The rest will be left behind.

Is it true?

"Is there any one of you who owns a hundred sheep and one of them gets lost, who wouldn't leave the ninety-nine in the wilderness, and go after the one that got lost until he finds it? And when he finds it, he lifts it upon his shoulders, happy. Once he gets home, he invites his friends and his neighbors over, and says to them, Celebrate with me, because I have found my lost sheep." Luke 15:4-6

This parable, the way Jesus taught to indicate just how committed God responds to Its creation, says celebrate when the lost are found. Jesus lived his life teaching gratitude, forgiveness and love: The elements of a good life. You can't live a double life enslaved by fear, trying to be happy.

When we get lost, who seeks to find us? Who goes looking for the lost soul? I find it too easy to ignore my lost friends. I struggle with myself to make sure I am available to those who are lost in a world they find hostile and dissimilar from what they used to know. I am not Mother Theresa. I am Dr. Jim, a minister with many years of experience praying that I may always be of service to those attracted to my being. I trust that I am willing and receptive to the highest ideal of love.

Jesus didn't care if you were a Jew, Gentile, or Roman.

"God causes the sun to rise on both the bad and the good, and sends rain on both the just and the unjust." Matthew 5:45

Jesus did care about those who felt lost, worried about death, status, or condition. The words Jesus shares, "...the sun rises on both the bad and the good," ring in my ear and call me out.

This Way of Jesus, this Cause and Effect world dominated by dominators throws my world out of balance. This now, in which I am, knows me only in accord with what I am, the product of what I believe. That which lines up with my experience turns either my fear on or my peace on. What binds me to the world? Am I living in choice or in default?

The Sacred Voice of Transformation

A sacred voice within speaks to each of us in the language of Universal Love...inviting us to believe, accept, and receive the life we were created to live. Its eternal power and glory never abandons us. It animates our lives and provides whatever is necessary to fulfill our greatest desire. It is a voice of transformation that cannot be erased or removed from our being.

But a problem exists!

NOT EVERYONE LISTENS!

Many are called by the voice of love, but fear—disguised as reason and common sense—yells danger, danger, danger...faith is not enough; prayer is not reliable; you are not worthy; you haven't earned it; and God's watching you!

Are you junk? Why would God create junk? Every creation is a work of art designed to contribute and deliver a life that wants to live.

Why would God create you and then punish you for being yourself? Traditional science and religion have, for centuries, tried to cast doubt on artists, intellectuals, homosexuals, writers, poets and spiritual leaders—labeling them as unacceptable in God's eye. But God doesn't see status, station or preference: God only sees the person. And in God's eyes, all are sacred.

> *"No one lights a lamp and then puts it in a cellar..." Luke 11:33*

Every creation moves along a pathway of discovery. Humanity calls this path growth; science calls it evolution; philosophy calls it wisdom; religion calls it revelation. No matter what you call the path, the human mind defines the path and itself by the complexities of its ever-evolving story. Those who cannot see the hidden meaning in their stories remain trapped in a field of space-time unable to transform — incapable of forgiveness or gratitude.

Those who are mentally stuck in a space-time world explain beauty by comparing it to what's ugly, measure peace by the absence of war, manipulate love by trying not to hate, and analyze light by contemplating darkness.

When humanity heads in this direction of comparison, it focuses on *what it doesn't want* and is, ironically, doomed to repeat the experience of *what it doesn't want*. This is because what you think about all day long, you tend to attract.

I have listened to these stories for over 34 years and helped people understand the Law of Attraction — that what they focus on they repeat. The irony, humanity as a whole has memorized how to be a victim, and victims pay attention to what they don't want. Consciously or unconsciously, this attention to feelings and thoughts of being a victim recreates the experience.

The Way of Jesus works to solve the problem of victim thinking because it goes right to your potential and unlocks the door with a minimum of fanfare or explanation. Why are you in trouble, in debt, lonely, or feeling powerless? The answer as to why is not as important as to what.

What matters? Focus on your good and take the path revealed. Follow the path revealed, a never-ending advancement that takes you deeper and deeper into the Infinite Presence, a spiritual transformation that eclipses the human form of God and helps each to mature.

Transformation, the product of spiritual discipline, requires listening, affirmative prayer and a willingness to stay focused on the idea of basic goodness until it manifests. Many people live in the distracted voice of tradition.

The Voice of Tradition

The voice of traditional Science and Religion dismisses The Way of Jesus and the Law of Attraction because it doesn't fight for peace, declare war on hate or drugs, or endlessly analyze depression to understand happiness.

The traditional voice of Science and Religion calls The Law of Attraction dangerous and the desire for more material satisfaction shallow and vain.

Bet you won't see a lot of the traditional voices of medicine, academia, religion or journalism rejecting their station, status or wealth; nor do they consider themselves shallow or vain for having achieved their goals.

Did not a vision of success inspire them to accomplish their dreams? Did they go into their chosen fields to be poor and unsuccessful? What attracted their blessings? Did their egocentric nature convince them life came from fate, fortune or fame?

The same voice that called them—through the Law of Attraction—is calling you. Are you listening to what you want or are you listening to the story of why you are limited?

If you are listening to the complexities of humanity's ever-evolving soap opera—trapped in a field of space-time—trying to explain your feelings of despair and doubt, your harvest will be limited. *Time-worn* and *space-tested*...human stories of failure and rejection are reruns of the same episodes you have experienced and watched all your life.

If you break the spell of these monotonous episodes, the world calls you dangerous and superficial for wanting a better life.

The Way of Jesus succeeds because it simplifies the complexities of life by streamlining all of life into one very basic idea: It's done unto you AS you believe. This is the Law of Attraction reduced to one word: AS.

Science wants to find the Theory of Everything. Religion wants to prove it's right by making everyone else wrong. Humanity remains stuck in the middle wanting to look good, act accordingly, and be on the right side. But, no matter what, the world still operates on three words: AS YOU BELIEVE.

Do not confuse this with positive or negative thinking. This basic truth, as you believe, works because it can be applied, measured, repeated and observed.

The Voice of Love

Those who don't know Love are boxed in by penalties and rules, punished for being themselves, rejected for relying on a power that created their lives based on how they perceive their place in the world, left behind because they didn't see value in the traditions of those who would exclude the dreamers and the visionaries.

The world offers one answer for the dreamer: NO WAY!

But the Way of Jesus and the Universe suggests a different answer: WAY!

The Way of Jesus emancipates those who understand, engaging them to live a different life. For those who've studied the law, the Way of Jesus is like the ever-elusive pickle jar in the refrigerator of life. You can open the door and stare right at the pickles and not see them. WHAT'S THAT ABOUT?

What you want lives right before your eyes. Nonetheless, if your eyes are in the back of your head looking at the past or caught up speculating about the future, you will not see what you want. You will only see where you have been or where you do not want to go.

The Way of Jesus makes *what you love* the focal point of your existence and relies on it to lead and guide you to a greater life. The Law of Attraction is impersonal; it responds to your core belief. The Way of Jesus teaches you to focus on love as the most desirable quality of life.

Allow yourself to be a magnet powered with love, forgiveness and gratitude. Develop your ability to speak love, forgiveness and gratitude. Work on your mental vocabulary, seeing yourself having what you want and every experience leading you to where you want to go.

The Voice of Self-Absorption

The disease of the twenty-first century is SELF-ABSORPTION. When you are self-absorbed you say things like, "Why is this happening to me?" The conditions and circumstances suck you in and hold your mind captive. You use the details of your "condition to make up stories to justify your repeated feelings of helplessness. You struggle to think proactive because you're convinced that until your problems are solved you won't know success.

Self-centered, exclusive, and in need of instant gratification, you get lost in the search for solutions, locked in a feeling of separation and fear. Being left behind, the human consequence dressed in religious clothing becomes the mental driver that keeps reaching into the subconscious looking for the answer to a problem that doesn't exist.

This misconception misdirects your mind and sets up an expectation that traps you in this ridiculous assumption.

Traditional religion and science want to confront conditions and go to war, doing battle to win their place, change the outcome, or improve their lot.

Traditional religion and science stay focused on the details absorbed in the feelings and thoughts, that appear to be the cause of our inadequacy. People seek ways to overcome the invisible emotional energy that opposes their advance.

Ask a doctor why you're not getting better and they are likely to say, "You need a different drug" or "Research is being done—be patient."

Ask a minister why this is happening to you and they are likely to say, "It's God's will or God works in mysterious ways."

Feel left behind or left out?

111

The Way of Jesus becomes definite if you focus on what you want. Turn away from the condition. Build on your strengths and remember God does not take sides. The impersonal power of the Law of Attraction works through your core beliefs fueled by your deepest feelings. This is why you cannot afford to be absorbed in your conditions, problems, or circumstances. You must do the exercises that refocus your thoughts and bring your spiritual practice into alignment with your most PRODUCTIVE IDEAS.

Religion and Science walked away from each other during the Renaissance period. In the 13th century, Western Religion took the path of idealism while science took the path of pragmatism. They both became absorbed in their models and vigorously defend their real estate in the arena of human attention.

The Law of Attraction becomes a bridge that can span the gap created by division and uncertainty. You must learn to use the Law in a constructive manner, with a high moral sense of doing *good*. The Way of Jesus will not operate in a get-rich-quick scheme. The Way of Jesus, a definite process of peace, requires a definite approach.

The Voice of Expectation Versus Expectancy

There is a difference between expectancy and expectation. Expectation is a need to have something turn out in a specific way, as in, I want that particular house, or I want that particular car, or I want that particular person—and nothing else will make me happy.

Expectation is a huge stumbling block when it comes to understanding The Law of Attraction. It is an important distinction and a big reason why many people have missed the message of Jesus and turned Christianity into an exclusive tribe—members only.

Traditional Christians often quote Jesus as having said in John 5:22:

"Not that the Father condemns anyone; rather, he has turned all such decisions over to the son, so that everyone will honor the son, just as they honor the Father. Whoever does not honor the son does not honor the Father who sent him."

This type of authority, according to many scholars, is not the words of Jesus. But rather, "a kind of boasting that contravenes (disregards) the image projected by the Jesus who warns his disciples that those who seek to be first will be last and that those who promote themselves will be demoted. Rather than authentic words of Jesus, the author of the Fourth Gospel (John) presents his own meditations

113

on the theological significance of Jesus." (the Five Gospels)

Such statements accepted as the truth automatically turn Jesus into a gatekeeper and heaven into a human country club managed by penalties, rules, and doctrine. This is not Jesus. It is more like a tribal version of Jesus, setting expectations for human behavior that qualify and quantify each according to the judgments of how well you followed the rules and kept yourself in line. This sets an expectation of failure which constantly sees humanity as trying to please Jesus.

Jesus had no expectation for humanity. Jesus' attitude animated his sense of *expectancy*; that each of us would find the truth and set ourselves free from a consciousness of failure and success, sin and punishment, dogma and disappointment, to the degree that we could see our blessings, imagine a greater good, and behave as if our lives were in a constant state of coming true.

Expectations are the root of superstition because expectations promote a belief in a worldly supernatural power that can fix or control outcomes. Expectations do this by validating a life defined by failure and success that inevitably leads to a false and misguided idea that winning could be more important than being alive.

Traditional Christianity teaches this kind of expectation because Christian fundamentalists view Jesus as a supernatural force who stands at heaven's gate and checks to see if you're a Christian. What if heaven, a state of mind and not a place, showed us the Way of Jesus that taught by example?

What if consciousness opens and closes the gate to happiness, that you can lay your life down or pick it up at will? What if spiritual freedom lived in our faith and did not discriminate, ever?

No one fails when they operate at the frequency of Love. All action taken in the name of Love eventually results in a greater good. Never judge the outcome according to your expectations, but according to your sense of *expectancy* that—no matter what happens—you can trust the Law of Attraction. It always works according to the thoughts and feelings you hold at the core of your being.

What makes expectancy hard or easy? Consider this statement, which most scholars believe Jesus did say:

"When you are about to appear with your opponent before the magistrate, do your best to settle with him on the way, or else he might drag you up before the judge, and the judge turn you over to the jailer, and the jailer throw you in prison.

I tell you, you'll never get out of there until you've paid every last red cent." Luke 12:58

These are tough words about the Law of Attraction, and how the Law says you must right yourself in the eyes of the only judge that matters: YOUR OWN CONSCIENCE. Guilt, shame, blame, and fear are all self-imposed nightmares. They are not penalties; they are consequences for living in the expectation that the world holds the answer to your success. A deep resentment or disappointment can hypnotize us to the point where, when the world says, "you're a chicken," guess what? You tend to act like a chicken!

What will it take to settle the disputes and injuries of the world?

Go ahead. Make that treasure map. Put a face on that vision. Fill your heart with light and love. We call this living in Expectancy, The Way of Jesus, the highest signal you can send. Once you start to live the dream, you wake up to God's Reality and the world transforms. If your desires seem shallow or materialistic at first, don't be concerned. As you grow and prove the Law of Attraction works, your trust in the Universe will mature from childish to childlike.

"When I was a child, I spoke as a child, I felt as a child, I thought as a child. Now that I have

become a man (human), I have put away childish things." Corinthians 13:11

One of my favorite quotes from the Bible is not attributed to Jesus but was said by Paul.

"How privileged are the eyes that see what you see! I tell you, many prophets and kings wanted to see what you see, and didn't see it, and hear what you hear, and didn't hear it." Luke 10:23

Jesus kept saying, "Get eyes and get ears." The Way of Jesus wants you to see the truth within and begin to live the life God created you to live.

The INCLUSIVE nature of Jesus resists those who try to keep him exclusive. The Way of Jesus claims no special privilege. Anyone who thinks this way will awaken one day and find themselves surrounded by and inseparably part of a greater whole. When that day comes for them, they will see that no one is left behind and no one can ever be excluded from God's love. The intelligence of God could not create such a nightmare.

Chapter 8
Stories of Love and How Love Works

Corinthians 13:1-13 on love, translated into the Way of Jesus and the Law of Love

~ Corinthians 1 ~

¹If I speak with the languages of men and of angels, but don't have love, I have become sounding brass, or a clanging cymbal.

Today, The Law of Love silences my anger, frustration, and expectations. I serve the Law. The Law serves me.

Why do we think that words spoken without the intention to express love will communicate love?

In 1984, I stopped teaching music. Two years before, I had reached a crisis in my professional life. Burned out and not happy, my life felt and tasted like a stale donut. I lost my way and went to see my minister for counseling.

We talked about change. How attitude and faith played a critical role in my transition to another line of work. I struggled because I loved my students, but did not love my routine.

Rev. Leslie said, "You must bring your job teaching music to completion and prepare your work to be handed to another so your students could transition without any sense of disruption to the learning environment." In other words, prepare ye the way! Love those kids and make sure you hand them to a teacher who could also love and lead them.

This information changed my mind and inspired a miracle. I returned to my classroom and began to see my students as a reflection of my dedication and commitment. I prepared myself for change and began the search for what I wanted to do.

I did not see or use the Law of Love in my transformation from teacher to minister. How could I forget my love of kids and my love of teaching? My ego was clanging the cymbals and sounding the brass, intoxicating my mind with guilt. I disconnected from unconditional love and lost my sense of trust. It took two years to readjust my attitude and find the right person to give me the space to create my next move, two years of love dedicated to my kids in preparation to hand off my work to another, two years to search for what I wanted to do.

~ Corinthians 2 ~

[2]If I have the gift of prophecy, and know all mysteries and all knowledge; and if I have all faith, so as to remove mountains, but don't have love, I am nothing.

Today, I am something because Love moves me to a higher plane beyond the mystery of worldly knowledge.

There have been times in my career as a minister that I did not know if the church could pay the rent and pay me. My first three years of doing ministry I took over a church in Florida and used my teacher retirement to supplement my income.

In 1987, I left Florida and returned to Southern California to start a church in Costa Mesa. This time I didn't have any retirement to fall back on and my small congregation could not support me in my new ministry.

I had prophesied and felt I had the faith necessary to grow and be able to afford our meeting place and my small salary. It worked for a while and then the mountain got bigger and no matter how much I worried, it wouldn't move. Fear began to creep into my thinking and I forgot the purpose of my ministry. It was time to talk with my Creator.

"God," I said, "I don't know how to move this mountain but I know how to do my job, and my job description did not include worry. So, God, I need you to do your job, and I commit to stop being afraid and trust that you know how to pay the rent and my salary."

I got up the next day and, for an instant, I felt a little fear trying to work its way back into my feeling nature. "Fear," I said, "You are not welcome here. I have important work to do and I intend to love my work and myself." Within two days, all the money necessary to pay the rent and my salary showed up in the bank.

I am nothing without love and I am nothing without God's love. My language and my angels now express love and my life feels the blessing.

~ Corinthians 3 ~
3If I give away all I have, and if I deliver up my body to be burned,but have not love, I gain nothing.

In this moment, I see the wisdom of acceptance and love. I refuse to sacrifice my life, and I chose to live life with love as my guide.

Acceptance and love are two of the most important spiritual qualities I work on every day. My mental work aims at the way I think and feel.

For example, this morning my wife did not feel well. I got up, got dressed, hooked up the dogs, put two doggie bags in my jacket and started out the door—not happy about having to walk the dogs. Half way down the street, I started to monitor my feelings and the way my thought directed my sense of acceptance. My internal mind said, *pay attention to how the negative nullifies your ability to think a higher thought.*

The way of my ego wanted me to give up my sense of peace and focus on my resentment. I noticed how I walked and fumed at my predicament. I thought to myself, *if I let this attitude persist, I am not going to have a good day. I have to let it go and embrace the moment and begin to love the walk, the dogs, the mission, and my wife.*

When I got back to the house, my mind focused on acceptance and my heart on love. I remember my affirmation, "I am grateful for my life and the opportunity to be of service to my wife and our dogs."

This may seem like a little thing, until you conjure up the consequences of the negative way my mind was moving. Negativity ruins your day. It casts a shadow on everything you think, do and experience. It casts a shadow on your work and your relationships. It can be difficult to detect the shadow. It blends so well with every experience, person, place and condition you run into.

Affirm: *In this moment, I see the wisdom of acceptance and love. I refuse to sacrifice my life to negativity. I chose to live life with love as my guide.*

~ Corinthians 4 ~
[4]*Love is patient and is kind; love doesn't envy. Love doesn't brag, is not proud*

Today I am patient, kind, and see all as one. All is Love and all is Law.

The simplicity of our teaching and the beauty of how Principle defines me figures into the equation of how I live in peace. Eight years into my ministry, I trained four ministers and my ego took a victory run up the ladder in my organization. People didn't know the importance of my work, but I did.

My pride disconnected me from God. My ego connected me with my accomplishment in grooming one of my new ministers to go out of state and take over a church.

We had a fundraiser for this minister and she planned to sell her condominium and move to the state of Washington in two months. We seeded her over $4,000 and celebrated her new move with a party. Months went by and my minister-student kept making excuses that no one seemed interested in buying her condominium.

Then I got the call. My newly-trained minister changed her mind. She decided to start a new church in my neighborhood and about a third of our members were going with her. I felt betrayed and angry. I did not feel like being kind or patient and my upset went on for a good six months. I am embarrassed to reveal that during my six months of disappointment I had failed to call any of my minister friends for prayer or counsel, intoxicated with self-righteous indignation.

Then it happened. I called a minister friend and asked her to pray to help me heal my disappointment and return to loving my ministry and myself. Within 24 hours, I possessed a new understanding about my work and the importance of my focus. I changed my mind about my former ministerial student and released her and everyone who left with her.

I no longer hold back in asking for prayer work. I am no longer proud. I am in love with love.

~ Corinthians 5 ~
5doesn't behave itself inappropriately, doesn't seek its own way, is not provoked, takes no account of evil;

Today, I am in harmony with my surroundings, moving on a path of cooperation, invoking the Law of Attraction by seeing only the good.

I have come to a personal belief about disappointment. The inappropriate nature of my disappointments are an unconscious choice that overwhelms how I feel. Disappointment wastes huge amounts time and disrupts my ability to be of service. Disappointment takes away my desire to serve; and if I try to be of service, my disappointment makes my service feel like a sacrifice.

None of this helps me love or even feel loved. This doesn't mean I don't experience disappointment. It means that disappointment is an unconscious choice provoked by backward thoughts. The sooner I catch it and redirect my thought, the better off I am.

A while ago, I worked on a committee to bring together two organizations that had split apart over 50 years ago. The committee had worked for seven years to find common ground; and we were building a bridge across a deep gulley of distrust and lots of disappointments. We knew the work ahead of us and we were committed to another few years of bridge building when suddenly the organizations disbanded our committee, skipped the bridge building and jumped in bed. Did I react? Yes!

No matter how long I study the Way of Jesus, if I get disappointed; I go into another universe.

My condition cheated, disrespected, and then dismissed me. I suffered under this illusion until I worked my way back to love and saw the circumstances in light of the changes I needed to make, but resisted.

Now, when that kind of circumstance emerges, I stand back and affirm, *lead me not into temptation but deliver me from error*. In the figure below, you can see the Aramaic pronunciation. (Dr. Rocco Errico's translation)

and let not	OO-LA
us enter	TA-LAN
into temptation	EL-NIS-YO-NA
but	EL-LA
part us	PA-SAN
from (error) evil	MEN BEE-SHA

~ Corinthians 6 ~
*[6]doesn't rejoice in unrighteousness, but
rejoices with the truth;*

*Today, I rejoice in the power of love and seek to know the
truth love clarifies.*

Politics is not easy when you are committed to
living in Principle, the Way of Jesus. When I see
injustice, I react from a memory forged in the '60s
and nurtured by a lifetime of activism. I believe in
civil rights, and I react when I see racism raise its ugly
head in our country. My reactions, while
understandable, are not productive.

As a minister, I cannot afford to take righteous
stands. Instead, I take a stand for Love and seek to
love even those I—by mistake—judge as
incompetent or reckless. When I celebrate my
righteousness, I separate myself from God and those
who really need my love. This isn't easy. I love my
righteousness. It makes me drunk on my opinions
and keeps me from doing my work—and yes, mental
hangovers happen.

This doesn't mean I don't act. It means that I don't
hate those I don't agree with. Love, a local experience
fostered by a commitment to listen and let go of my
judgments, functions in favor of a bigger truth. This
reassures me that all conditions are temporary and in

constant transition. In other words, life combines constant change with no permanence, which requires huge amounts of patience while we wait for God to reveal all.

It takes persistence to discover and correct your own prejudice, to change the way you think and the way you live. The Way of Jesus will not allow you to live in prejudice for long. The consequence, not visible, takes a toll on everyone in your life. Your anger, your fear, and your hate, cannot hide for long.

In the early 90s, the term feminism captured my attention, the result of an embarrassing experience of sharing what I thought was a joke with a gay woman friend.

She listened and was offended and that caught me off guard. We talked and I saw my prejudice, unforgiveable, shallow, and insensitive. Soon after that experience, I saw in the local paper an announcement of a Goddess Festival of Alters presented at a local Women's Center held in West Los Angeles. I went and pivoted to a radical change of heart.

I drove 35 miles to see this Goddess Festival of Alters. The Center, not easy to find, located in a residential area, hidden among normal looking houses, did not stand out. This tested my resolve to find the feminine presence disguised as a residence, not a building of note.

This revelation exposed within my perception a blind spot, of which I had no experience or personal knowledge. I compare it to the phenomena of the South American Indians who, when they first saw the white sails of the Spanish explorers, thought they were clouds carrying the Gods. It took time to fill in the blank spot in my mental drawer called women, a good place to start, The Goddess Festival of Alters. They displayed over twelve different alters and each had a unique piece of information of how women saw the Divine.

I had no idea about the treasure I had discovered. Could this be the Way of Jesus? No, the Way of the Goddess shared the Love of the Goddess, which did not look the same compared with the Love of God. This discovery exposed my incompetency and excited my curiosity. For in the end I had found the missing piece of humanity hidden from my view until I was ready to find what was absent from my point of view. Corinthians 6 says, doesn't rejoice in unrighteousness, but rejoice with the truth.

Today, I rejoice in the power of love and gladly seek to know the truth love clarified in me when I discovered the Goddess I yearned to understand. My unrighteousness no longer occupies the center of my attention. Instead, I rejoice with a newfound truth that compliments and helps to complete my humanity.

~ Corinthians 7 ~
[7]bears all things, believes all things, hopes all things, endures all things.

Today Love bears all that would distract or discourage me from moving to the higher ground of perfect life, perfect love, perfect being.

I remember the times when Love pivoted in my favor. In 1962, while a junior in high school, I won a scholarship to a music camp hosted by a very prestigious university.

For two weeks I worked with some of the best music teachers in the world. They inspired me in so many ways. One moment stands out.

One afternoon, on a large rock next to the art studio overlooking the open-air performance theater, I listened to the university brass choir play Aaron Copland's, *Fanfare for the Common Man.* Written in 1942, four-years before I arrived on the planet, I sat on that rock, seventeen years old, tears rolling down my cheeks, thinking, *I want to do that.*

Since then, I have documented my *love pivots.* The times and experiences that inspired me to change direction and live the Way of Jesus. I consider these moments as gifts from my creator that led me in the direction of what matters—to where I am today.

~ Corinthians 8 ~
[8]Love never fails. But where there are prophecies, they will be done away with. Where there are various languages, they will cease. Where there is knowledge, it will be done away with.

Today, all of my need to predict, control or study the problem is dismissed. Today, Love is sufficient unto Love.

I don't know anyone who loves failure; and I don't know anyone who doesn't love success. Both are the same. Both are the product of how we compare ourselves to others. I often tell my congregation that the only real sin is compare-a-sin (Comparison). Truth tells a different story: Winners, are in fact, losers in disguise who try to sustain their status. This does not represent the Way of Jesus.

When you label another a loser, you've identified them based on another who you call a winner. You can't have a loser without a winner or a winner without a loser. I know I am being redundant but Corinthians says that while love never fails, those who are addicted to forecasting the future, speaking many languages, or trying to acquire knowledge will eventually disappear, so too will winners and losers disappear. Eventually you stop competing and refocus your attention on Love.

When my son started high school, he tried out for the football team. His small skinny build could not compete. He didn't stand a chance with kids twice his size.

We talked. He complained. I suggested he quit and join the choir. He said no, because his friends would call him a quitter and a loser. He said he wanted to stick it out until the end of the semester and then he would go into choir.

He did stick it out until the end of the semester. Then he transferred into choir and started playing the guitar.

Fast forward 22 years and now, he plays professionally and writes his own music. Once he found his calling with his love of the guitar, his love of life expanded. As I frequently say, "All things come to pass."

Failure and success are what we walk through on our way to competency.

~ Corinthians 9 ~
⁹For we know in part, and we prophesy in part;

*Today, I align my worldly mind with God's Intelligence
and all that is partial becomes whole.*

Life is a whole experience even if you can only see part of it. Dr. Ernest Holmes, the author of The *Science of Mind*, wrote about the difference between having faith in God and having the faith *of* God.

Dr. Holmes asked, "Why must we believe? Because God is belief. God is belief and belief is Law, and Law produces form, in substance."

"When Jesus explained to his disciples that they had failed to heal because of a lack of faith, they protested that they did have faith *in* God. Jesus explained to them that this was insufficient; that they must have the faith *of* God. *The faith of God* acts in a different way from *a faith in God*. The faith of God IS God, and somewhere along the line of our spiritual evolution this transition will gradually take place, and we shall cease having faith IN and shall have the faith OF. We must believe because God is belief; the physical Universe, built out of belief, faith, acceptance, and conviction, awaits our vision." Science of Mind, Dr. Ernest Holmes, page 317

We disconnect from our faith OF God because the partial sense of being a whole person, while dealing with the doubt of not *feeling* whole, challenges our cultural values.

We prophesy in part, desperately trying to control the way life turns out. Life can only be for us to the degree that we believe in THE LIFE WE'VE BEEN GIVEN TO LIVE.

If I asked you, "How much of your life do you believe in?" Can you honestly say, "All of it?"

We prophesy in part because we slice our world into pieces to control it. We call this compartmentalization. We do not feel complete, and we don't know what to do about how that feels. While the dilemma has no answer, it does have a solution that creates a consciousness where the dilemma cannot exist.

It "starts with the premise that God is perfect, the Spiritual System is perfect, and we are part of this Spiritual System," and therefore, *spiritual man* is perfect. We must seek to disentangle our imagination from the material human experience and join our contemplation with the *spiritual human.*

The last hitch in this kiddy-up shows up in our concept of Time. The truth that solves this dilemma lives in THE TIMELESS NATURE OF SPIRIT. We have the power to transcend time and turn away from *any* form born of time's limitations. Our job is MENTAL. We must form a mental relationship with our Creator by loving God as God Loves Us: unconditional, timeless and without limitation.

~ Corinthians 10 ~

[10]*But when that which is complete has come, then that which is partial will be done away with.*

Today, I dismiss any idea of my life as partial or incomplete; my life is created in the image of a whole and complete idea of God.

I love this saying because when you see the BIG picture, you will not remember the partial idea you had of yourself. We possess the power of consciousness to the degree that we accept our freedom to imagine all that would serve our highest and best good.

The common belief among those seeking to GET rich falls into the category of consuming and hording their good. Locked in a belief of scarcity, the consumer works to manage the feeling of limitation by creating boundaries around their field of potential and their resources. While this gives them the feeling that they are protecting their wealth, the truth looks more as if they are withholding their wealth or keeping it out of circulation.

When that which is complete has come, they will give their wealth for a different kind of richness — the opportunity to be of service.

If you withhold your love, why would you expect a return on an investment you withheld? Perhaps you mistook your willingness to give, as a way to get, or as a way to receive what you think you *deserve*.

The old saying, "Don't let the right hand know what the left hand is doing," applies because once you give to get, you miss the point of your existence. You are here to SERVE AND TO BE SERVED. You are here because you have been given another opportunity to share and circulate your left-hand sharing and your right hand circulating, with no expectation of getting. You live to circulate your good back into humanity as a way of showing gratitude for life's gifts.

~ Corinthians 11 ~

11When I was a child, I spoke as a child, I felt as a child, I thought as a child. Now that I have become a man, I have put away childish things.

Today I celebrate my ability to see as a spiritual adult. Child-Like in my ability to see the truth...whole, perfect and complete.

The Way of Jesus appeals to those who maintain their sense of trust and innocence.

Judgment, a *parent-like* behavior, initiates immature and childish reactions.

Recently I interviewed Deepak Chopra on a radio program about his book, *You Are the Universe*. I knew that Chopra received a lot of criticism from classically-trained physicists because he dared to use spiritual philosophy to explain Einstein's theory of Relativity and Quantum Physics. I asked him how that felt. His answer reflected the Way of Jesus.

He said, "At first I felt angry and then I realized what an immature behavior anger manifests. I decided to stop being angry and take the time to stay in the conversation with those who could not accept my ideas. Now I have become good friends with some of my harshest critics."

This story always reminds me of a passage from Henry David Thoreau's book on *Walden Pond*.

"I went to the woods because I wished to live deliberately, to front only the essential facts of life, and see if I could not learn what it had to teach, and not, when I came to die, discover that I had not lived. I did not wish to live what was not life, living is so dear; nor did I wish to practice resignation, unless it was quite necessary. I wanted to live deep and suck out all the marrow of life, to live so sturdily and Spartan-like as to put to rout all that was not life, to cut a broad swath and shave close, to drive life into a corner, and reduce it to its lowest terms..."

There are a number of points in this story that reflect Thoreau's personal growth. The woods represent the life we avoid living, the life that calls us into the world of the *unknown* and confronts us with our potential—*the essential facts*. These are the challenges, the life experiences we must live through to discover the purpose and meaning of our lives. If you do not fully engage your purpose and meaning, you die debilitated with regret and remorse.

Live fully engaged. Never give up. Suck out all the marrow of life and live committed to your personal and timeless growth.

The personal story that follows shows the sequence and script of the Law of Attraction and how it responds to desire.

I started taking piano when I was 7 years old, and for seven years I toiled learning piano the same way I learned to type. It was all mechanics. I had no idea how the music worked or how I could stray from the printed notes and do my own thing.

When I was 14, I asked for a new piano teacher. I wanted to learn jazz. My mom found an older slim teacher who wore a wool suit in the summer with a white shirt, vest, and suspenders, and who chain-smoked Lucky Strike cigarettes. It was 1959, and I just wanted to be cool.

Eddie's studio was downtown on the second floor of an old brick building. The narrow stairway felt like a secret passageway. I opened the door. Eddie was in the recording booth cutting the master for a new 45 he was preparing to sell at Sears. The machine was big and dark with a pointed needle cutting a groove in a blank record. Eddie's head was down looking at the groove the machine cut in the blank record. "Have a seat at that piano. I'll be with you in a minute."

I turned around and saw the old upright piano. I walked over to the piano bench and, with my eyes still fixated on that machine, sat down. Eddy turned off the machine. It whined to a stop. Eddy walked over, sat down on the chair next to me and lit another Lucky Strike. I looked up and saw the other cigarette he placed on top of the piano.

"Do you know if you're sitting at the piano correctly?" I looked back and said, "I'm sitting in front of it."

"Bend your head over and tell me what key your nose hits?"

My nose hit the "f" key, four notes above middle "c." "Slide down about three keys and you will be in the center of the piano. That's important."

As I slid to my left, Eddy asked, "Can you spell ace?"

"A-C-E," I replied.

"Can you spell it with the "C" on the bottom?"

I was quiet. I did not know what he meant.

"There are three ways spell the "a" minor chord A-C-E, C-E-A, and E-A-C." In less than three minutes Eddy had taught me the "a" minor chord with the first two inversions and showed me how that chord lived on the piano and how to play it.

However, I learned more than that from Eddy that day. Just as Eddy finished explaining the "a" minor chord, he snuffed out his cigarette in the butt-packed ashtray. Without looking, Eddy reached up and flipped the unlit cigarette on top of the piano, caught it in his mouth and reached into his vest pocket, pulled out a Zippo lighter, flipped it open and in *one motion,* lit that cigarette at the same time it hit his lips. I thought, *I want to learn how to do that!*

What Eddy taught me gave me confidence in being a musician. What The Way of Jesus teaches me gives me confidence in the life I live. In both cases, my performance improved.

When my life performance lacks inspiration, I ask myself:

1. Are you sitting correctly in front of your potential?
2. Do you understand the power of your faith?

3. Are you ready to put away judgment and see the Divine in all?

~ Corinthians 12 ~

For now we see in a mirror, dimly, but then face to face. Now I know in part, but then I will know fully, even as I was also fully known.

Today I use my faith to know that God loves me, nurtures me, and provides all that is required for my highest good.

Authenticity, a desirable trait of character, comes to those who look into the mirror. The ability to see yourself, even dimly, will always reveal your primordial reason to be alive. The vast affirmative lives in all of life and our consciousness reflects the image of how we conceive that affirmative. In other words, what we are looking for, we are looking with. This reflects more than sight or image. It reflects our experience, and it does it in a perfect three-dimensional form. This miracle, often overlooked and taken for granted, allows us to attach meaning and stimulate feelings that inform and inspire new ways of thinking.

In a Cause and Effect reality, we see what we believe. The Way of Jesus says, "It is done unto you as you believe." This affirmative statement defines the life we live. Since you can never experience more than you believe, you experience in part even though the power of the Divine within you knows in full. This explains the statement, "Now I know in part, but then I will know fully, even as I was also fully known."

Although we cannot hide our Divine Nature, we can disguise it, dress it up in anger, fear and uncertainty, and, for a while, pretend we do not know who we are. We can go on this way for a while, absorbed in our condition, unavailable to love or be loved. Nonetheless at some point, we will wake up and re-member and re-join who we are and be fully known.

Jesus became fully known, available in his authentic human form, teacher, healer, wisdom speaker. Jesus' Divine-Self reflected back to ALL who desired to be healed, the image of their life reflected as in a mirror, whole, perfect and complete.

This faith of God heals and restores our connection to our creator and lifts the spirit into that which can be known and reflect, for all who are willing to look, the image of unconditional love. This enables all who are receptive to being the healing agent of love, to be the Way of Jesus, the Way that reconciles the heart and mind and brings peace unto all.

~ Corinthians 13 ~

But now faith, hope, and love remain and of these three; the greatest of these is Love.

Today I am lead by faith, hope and love, but my greatest guide is Love.

In the Science of Mind, Dr. Ernest Holmes writes about faith and says, "Faith is a mental attitude which is so convinced of its own idea—which so completely accepts it—that any contradiction is unthinkable and impossible."

This *state of mind*, which Dr. Holmes says, "is so convinced of its own idea..." does not happen by accident. It happens because the Way of Jesus, acting through Love, elevates the way we think. This Way dismisses any thoughts or reactions contrary to the Way of Jesus and plants the seed of possibility ready to inter-act with the soil of our consciousness and grow into an experience of perfect love.

I do feel blessed by my opportunities and the people I know. They are my teachers and each has shown me how love functions and life changes.

The following story is taken from a book I wrote entitled, *When It's Time to Leave*, available on Amazon.com

When my father passed, my brother, sister, and I were all standing watch at the hospital. Dad's bladder did not work and internally nothing could pass. Uremic poisoning set in and we waited. He refused to give up. It was morning and I had to go to my office and take care of a few calls. My brother was with him and said, "Go ahead. I will watch." On my way back to the hospital, my bother called and said the train had left the station (this was code for Dad had passed).

My sister and I arrived at the same time and the three of us stood next to Dad's bed, held hands and said goodbye. We all cried and promised to take care of each other, and we have. That night my wife made us dinner and we ate and told stories of our youth. The miracle of a loving family who appreciated their parents.

Not all, of course, have had good memories about their parents. When this happens, the importance of *forgiveness* shows up. My wife Patty was estranged from her father for years and had witnessed him abuse her mother. We talked about the importance of forgiveness and how those who do not forgive tend to hang on to resentments and anger—that those memories can cause all kinds of internal strife and unhappinesss. She worked with a prayer partner and began to forgive her dad. One day, while working up the courage to call Dad, he called her. His son, my wife's half-brother, was getting married and he wanted her to come to the wedding. Miracles happen when your intention meets forgiveness and love guides the way, The Way of Jesus.

"There are only two ways to live your life. One is as though nothing is a miracle. The other is as though everything is a miracle."
– Albert Einstein

Chapter 9
Consider This

The Gift, The Opportunity, The Change

Life can be a very fragile gift. You have the opportunity to live it to the fullest and so you should.

Do not avoid your originality. Put aside the things that waste time or serve no real point in your development. You have talents, skills, and other gifts. Make sure you use them every day to advance your growth. Do not let them lie dormant. Your gifts have meaning and are central to the life God created you to live.

You will find the meaning to who you are in the world of Principle. A world where you apply meaning and unveil truth. The world itself has no meaning except the meaning you give it. This includes people, places, jobs, careers and relationships.

If you get lost and can't find your way, stop, be still, breathe, and listen. God will tap you on the shoulder and remind you that all of life exists to give you a place to see, serve, and develop your being. Every gift given helps develop your amazing power to create the life you want to live. Even your so-called problems are nothing more than a temporary illusion easily corrected by focusing on what wants to happen by means of this life God created for you to grow into.

There are those who seem lost, but you do not have to be lost. The invisible presence of God works through everything. The blessing lives everywhere in everything. Claim it, believe it, then dismiss all doubt, disbelief, and fear that might stand in the way. You can create your success, but it must come by means of your thoughts and feelings. Life in this world orbits around the core desires of those who choose to live here and now.

Jesus lived his life in complete faith. He had no agenda other than to inform and inspire humanity to rise to a spiritual truth he forever pointed to and encouraged all to believe. He also practiced what he taught. When confused or in need of clarity, he would retreat to the desert and meditate. He had no real job. Even though some people portray him as a carpenter, no written account exists that he ever used that profession to make a living. In fact, he did not work in the conventional sense, but enjoyed a continuous supply of whatever he needed.

Does this signal us to stop working? No. It signals us to pay attention to what we want and make sure we focus on implementing our highest desires, interests and talents. We also must be disciplined in our approach to truth and use the principles presented to clarify our intentions in the action we take.

I took ownership of my life, the moment I discovered that I was a part of a Divine creation, created to live a prosperous life. No point in living in a consciousness of lack. The Way of Jesus lives within the Way I am and the Way I am lives within the Divine Idea of a Creative Mind in action. The timeless infinite and the unconditional nature of God are one. The form the Infinite takes lifts life into a new idea of love, ready to live the moment I am ready to trust.

I give thanks that my life and God's life are one in expression. I release my life into that Love and Peace God so brilliantly provides. The Way of Jesus lives in the now and so do I.

More programs by Dr. Jim Turrell

The Next Step Workshop is a 60 to 90-minute three-part presentation based on Dr. Jim's book, *When It's Time to Leave*. Perfect for boomers and their children and families with grandparents. You will learn:

1. The Nature of Death, a personal Transformation and a Cosmic Shove into a Greater Experience of Life.
2. Practical Tools that will prepare you for grief, death, fear, and the confusion that always accompanies the departure.
3. How to write yourself a eulogy and be present at your memorial.

Speaking from the Heart, a book I wrote in 1998 shows you how to compose and deliver an inspiring message WITHOUT NOTES. In this class, you will learn:

1. The benefit of a Story Telling Template
2. The Secret to Delivering a Message without notes or memorization.
3. How to emotionally connect with your audience

Contact Information for Dr. Jim Turrell
Email: jturrell@cslnm.org
Office Phone: 714 754-739

50632453R00094

Made in the USA
San Bernardino, CA
28 June 2017